Orders: Please contact How2become Ltd, Suite 2, 50 Churchill Square Business Centre, Kings Hill, Kent ME19 4YU.

You can order through Amazon.co.uk under ISBN 978-1-910602-40-9, via the website www.How2Become.com or through Gardners.com.

ISBN: 978-1-910602-40-9

First published in 2015 by How2become Ltd.

Typeset for How2become Ltd by Anton Pshinka.

Disclaimer

Every effort has been made to ensure that the information contained within this guide is accurate at the time of publication. How2become Ltd is not responsible for anyone failing any part of any selection process as a result of the information contained within this guide. How2become Ltd and their authors cannot accept any responsibility for any errors or omissions within this guide, however caused. No responsibility for loss or damage occasioned by any person acting, or refraining from action, as a result of the material in this publication can be accepted by How2become Ltd.

The information within this guide does not represent the views of any third party service or organisation.

how2become

Armed Forces
Tests

www.How2Become.com

As part of this product you also receive FREE access to online tests that will help you to pass the Armed Forces Tests.

To gain access, simply go to:

www.PsychometricTestsOnline.co.uk

Get more products for passing any test or interview at:

www.how2become.com

CONTENTS

INTRODUCTION
TO YOUR NEW GUIDE

INTRODUCTION TO YOUR NEW GUIDE

Welcome to your new guide, **Armed Forces Tests:** *Sample Tests for the Army, the Royal Air Force and the Royal Navy.*

Here at How2become, we have done our utmost to provide a guide packed full of hundreds of sample testing questions. This guide will be invaluable to anyone who wishes to successfully pass each stage of the Armed Forces application process.

Tasked with defence, the Armed Forces play a crucial role in the protection of our country. Joining the Armed Forces in any type of role will require hard work and determination. The selection tests used within the Armed Forces are designed to assess whether potential candidates have the *'ability'* to meet the demanding nature of life within the service.

The purpose of this book is to guide you through the psychometric tests used to join the Army, the RAF and the Royal Navy. It has been written with the intention of bettering your scores and improving your overall performance. Generally, the higher scores you achieve during the assessment, the more job opportunities you will have at your disposal. We guarantee you a professional guide, which will help you to fully grasp psychometric tests and assist you during your preparation period.

We would recommend that, no matter the job you are applying for – whether that be a job in the RAF, the Royal Navy or the Army, you practice ALL of the questions contained within this guide. You will find that the more practice you undertake in the build up to your test, the better you will perform on the day. Each testing chapter assesses similar skills and qualities, and therefore practising all of the questions in this guide can only better your chances of success.

If you are serious about joining the Armed Forces, you should do your utmost to prepare yourself for the selection process!

STRUCTURE OF THE GUIDE

In order to make the most out of your guide, we have formatted this book in a simple and clear structure, detailing all of the information and practice you will need if you wish to be successful.

The guide is broken up into three key sub-sections, each relating to the three different areas of the Armed Forces:

- **The British Army Recruit Battery Test (BARB);**
  - o *Information on BARB Test;*
  - o *Example questions;*
  - o *Testing sections comprising lots of sample questions;*
  - o *Detailed answers and explanations;*

- **The Royal Navy Recruiting Test (RN);**
  - o *Information on RN Test;*
  - o *Example questions;*
  - o *Testing sections comprising lots of sample questions;*
  - o *Detailed answers and explanations;*

- **The Royal Air Force Airman/Airwoman Selection Test (AST);**
  - o *Information on AST Test;*
  - o *Example questions;*
  - o *Testing sections comprising lots of sample questions;*
  - o *Detailed answers and explanations.*

We suggest that you begin with the testing section that you are applying for, and then if you wish to practice more questions, you can work through the rest of the guide. The questions are of similar style, so practising them all will only better your IQ and improve the 'essential' skills needed to successfully pass the selection process.

Good luck and best wishes.

The how2become team

The How2become team

PREFACE BY RICHARD MCMUNN

It's probably important that I start off by explaining a little bit about myself, my background, and why I'm suitably qualified to help you pass the selection tests that form part of the Armed Forces.

I left school at the usual age of 16 and joined the Royal Navy, serving on-board HMS Invincible as part of 800 Naval Air Squadron which formed part of the Fleet Air Arm. There I was at the age of 16, travelling the world and working as an engineer on Sea Harrier jets! It was fantastic and I loved every minute of it.

After four years, I left the Royal Navy and joined Kent Fire and Rescue Service as a Firefighter. Over the next 17 years, I worked my way up through the ranks to the position of Assistant Divisional Officer. During my time in the Fire Service, I spent a lot of time working as an instructor at the Fire Brigade Training Centre. I was also involved in the selection processes for assessing candidates who wanted to join the job as a Firefighter. Therefore, my knowledge and experience gained so far in life has been invaluable in helping people like yourself, to pass any type of selection process. I am sure you will find this guide an invaluable resource during your preparation period.

I have always been fortunate in the fact that I persevere at everything I do. I understand that if I keep working hard in life, then I will always be successful. This is an important lesson that I want you to take on-board straight away. If you work hard and persevere, then success will come your way.

Finally, it is very important that you believe in your own abilities. It does not matter if you have no qualifications. It does not matter if you are currently weak in psychometric testing. What does matter is *self-belief, self-discipline* and a *genuine desire to succeed*.

Best wishes,

Richard McMunn

Richard McMunn

ABOUT THE
ARMED FORCES

ABOUT THE ARMED FORCES

A career in the Armed Forces comes with a great deal of responsibility, commitment and integrity. It provides many career opportunities and is lucrative in terms of prospects, potential and earnings. That is why it is important that the Armed Forces employ people who show strong levels of enthusiasm and skill, in order to maintain a great level of service and professionalism.

Amidst the application process, you will be required to undergo a series of psychometric tests. These assessments have been used in the Armed Forces recruitment process for many years, and are used to primarily assess a candidates' suitability for specific job roles. Potential candidates need to understand the integrity and nature of the job, and be able to demonstrate the 'core competencies' to a high standard, in order to fulfil and meet the challenging criteria of life in the Armed Forces.

You will be assessed by undergoing a series of tests which illustrate how well you can perform specified tasks; tasks that test similar skills to the ones you will have to demonstrate in a real life situation. The selection processes will vary depending on whether you are applying for a position in the Army, the RAF or the Royal Navy, so it is important that you know what process you will be involved with, in order to successfully complete the psychometric stages of the assessment.

Each test used in the selection process is used for a particular reason. The level of difficulty for each test will also vary depending on the job position for which you are applying. Unsurprisingly, if you are going to be sitting a Royal Air Force assessment, this test is going to be noticeably more difficult as opposed to applying for a job in the Army. This is due to the roles in the RAF requiring a higher, more technical ability. Therefore it is vital that you improve your skills and performance by preparing as much as you can prior to your assessment.

ARMY – THE BRITISH ARMY RECRUIT BATTERY TEST (BARB TEST)

Since July 1992, as part of the Army selection process, you will be expected to undertake and pass an assessment called the *'British Army Recruit Battery Test'*; more commonly referred to as the *'BARB Test'*.

During this assessment, you will undergo five different tests, each used to assess different key skills and qualities required to join the Army. The test is used to measure a candidate's ability to interpret and understand information, and process that information in order to solve problems.

The five areas of the BARB Test include the following:

- *Reasoning Test* (12 questions);

- *Letter Checking Test* (16 questions);

- *Number Distance Test* (20 questions);

- *Odd One Out Test* (20 questions);

- *Symbol Rotation Test* (12 questions).

The test will be conducted on a computer, and comprise a series of timed assessments. After completing the assessment, the computer will automatically calculate your score, based on the number of correct answers and the time taken. The final score is referred to as the 'GTI' *(General Trainability Index)*, and will determine whether or not you have passed this part of the application process.

Ultimately, the higher the score, the more job opportunities you will have at your disposal.

The pass mark for the BARB Test is currently 26; although you will need to confirm this with your local Armed Forces Careers Office. This effectively means that you must get at least 26 questions correct in order to qualify. As I mentioned earlier, don't just settle for a minimum pass; you need to achieve as high a score as possible to ensure you are given more career opportunities.

ROYAL NAVY – THE ROYAL NAVY RECRUITING TEST (RT TEST)

The Royal Navy Recruiting Test (RT) will test your intellectual and academic ability, and therefore will provide a reflection on how well you are likely to perform in a specific role within the Royal Navy. It does not matter what qualifications you have, you will still be required to sit the RT, and your results will go towards determining your suitability for the Armed Forces. Your performance in the RT will demonstrate your ability to cope with the technical and academic requirements of working in the Royal Navy.

There are four separate parts of the test which you will need to complete and pass in order to move on to the next stage of the application process.

These tests will measure your levels of:

- *General Reasoning* (30 questions to be completed in 9 minutes);

- *Verbal Ability* (30 questions to be completed in 9 minutes);

- *Numerical Reasoning* (30 questions to be completed in 16 minutes);

- *Mechanical Comprehension* (30 questions to be completed in 10 minutes).

The tests are usually carried out at the Armed Forces Careers Office and will be taken under strict timed conditions. Details of the time restrictions and number of questions per exercise will be provided in your recruitment literature (the number of questions and time frame listed in the bullet points are correct at the time of publication). Your recruitment literature is key! Make sure that you take the time to read through the whole booklet, so that you are fully aware of what is expected during your assessment.

The pass mark for the Royal Navy Recruiting Test will very much depend on the technical level required for the post in which you are applying; although a pass mark of 50% is normally sufficient for the majority of branches.

ROYAL AIR FORCE – THE AIRMAN/AIRWOMAN SELECTION TEST (AST TEST)

The *Airman/Airwoman Selection Test (AST)* consists a number of different aptitude tests which are designed to assess which careers in the RAF are most suited to you. There are many different career opportunities available and each one will require a different level of skill.

The AST consists of seven aptitude tests as listed below:

- *A Verbal Reasoning Test* (15 minutes to answer 20 questions);

- *A Numerical Reasoning Test* (4 minutes to answer 12 questions on the first section. 11 minutes to answer 15 questions in the second section);

- *A Work Rate Test* (4 minutes to answer 20 questions);

- *A Spatial Reasoning Test* (4 minutes to answer 10 questions);

- *A Mechanical Comprehension Test* (10 minutes in which to answer 20 questions);

- *An Electrical Comprehension Test* (11 minutes to complete 21 questions);

- *A Memory Test* (There are two parts to this test and you will have a total of 10 minutes in which to answer 20 questions).

Now that we have taken the time to understand the different types of tests for the Army, Royal Navy or the Royal Air Force, you can undergo a prolonged period of practice questions.

Regardless of the service you are applying to join within the Armed Forces, it will be good practice to work through the sample tests for ALL three of the selection processes, to ensure that you are 100% prepared for your Armed Forces assessment.

British Army
Recruit Battery Test
(BARB)

WHAT IS THE BARB TEST?

If you are applying to join the Army, one of the initial stages during the selection process will require you to sit and pass the 'British Army Recruit Battery Test'; more commonly known as the 'BARB Test'.

WHO NEEDS TO TAKE THE BARB TEST?

If you are applying to join the Army, no matter what position or level, you will be required to complete the BARB Test.

WHY DO I NEED TO BE ASSESSED?

The BARB Test is primarily used to determine whether or not you make a suitable candidate for the Army. The test is used as a way of measuring your skills and qualities, and assess whether they match the competencies required by the Army. It is a tried and tested method that the Army uses to assess which career(s) you are most suited to. It is important that you aim for the highest score possible on the test to ensure yourself with the best range of opportunities regarding job prospects.

WHERE DO I TAKE THE TEST?

The assessment will most likely be held at an Army Careers Office.

WHAT DOES THE BARB TEST CONSIST OF?

If you are asked to sit a BARB Test, you should make yourself familiar with the contents of the assessment. During the assessment, you will be expected to answer numerous questions in a specified time frame. The types of questions are broken down into five key assessments:

- *Reasoning Test (12 questions);*
- *Letter Checking Test (16 questions);*
- *Number Distance Test (20 questions);*
- *Odd One Out Test (20 questions);*
- *Symbol Rotation Test (12 questions).*

TIPS FOR PASSING THE BARB TEST

- Undergo as much practice as you can. The more practice you undergo, the more competent you will become, thus improving your overall scores;

- Focus on the questions you struggle with first. Tackling the questions that you find most difficult will make sure that your weaker areas in the assessment have been revised and conquered;

- *Letter Checking Test* – when answering these types of questions, you may find it useful to scan each line downwards to check whether the letter is the same. You will have very little time during the real test, so you need to work as quickly and as accurately as possible. TOP TIP: Look out for letters that **look** similar but **are not** the same, such as *Q* and *O*, *G* and *Q*, *P* and *q*;

- *Odd One Out Test* – focus on how the words are connected. You may find that some words are the opposite of one another, or you may find that two words contain the same amount of syllables or letters. Find the connection between the words by working out how the words are linked;

- *Reasoning Test* – the more question types you practice, the better prepared you will feel. A TOP TIP is to repeat the statement at least twice before answering the question;

- *Number Distance Test* – the first step is to decide which of the three numbers is the smallest, and which is the biggest. Then look at the number you are left with, and decide if the smallest or biggest number is furthest away from the middle number. TOP TIP: Your answer will either be the smallest number or the biggest number; it will **never** be the middle number;

- *Symbol Rotation* – when you start practising these types of questions, you may find it difficult to visualise the shapes. A TOP TIP is to draw the symbols out yourself and rotate the paper; that way you can visually see where the symbols would be positioned;

- Practice your speed as well as your accuracy. Remember, the tests are timed, so you want to ensure that you have answered a sufficient amount of questions in the allotted time;

- Eliminate the most obscure answers first. This will save you time. By eliminating the answers you know to be incorrect, will narrow down the choices of possible correct answers.

WHAT DO THE QUESTIONS LOOK LIKE?

Below are example questions of the BARB Test. Look at the examples to see what types of questions you can expect to answer during your assessment.

REASONING

EXAMPLE 1

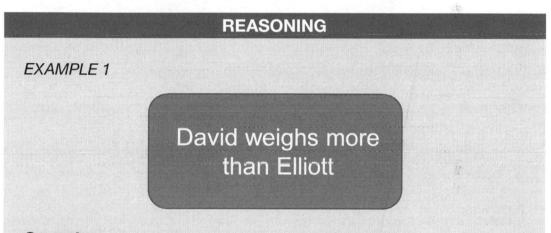

David weighs more than Elliott

Question

Who weighs less?

- TIP: Read the sentence in your head at least twice. This will make the question easier to answer;

- The statement is saying that David weighs the most, which means that Elliott must weigh less.

Answer

Elliott

REASONING

EXAMPLE 2

> Mia is not as tall as Gen

Question

Who is the tallest?

- TIP: Read the sentence in your head at least twice. This will make the question easier to answer;

- The statement is saying that Mia is not as tall as Gen, therefore Gen must be taller than Mia.

Answer

Gen

Things to remember:

- These questions are relatively simple. They do not require any knowledge or intellect;

- These questions do require you to read the statement carefully, and determine what the statement is *actually* saying;

- The key to these questions is **timing**. You need to ensure that you work as quickly as you can through these questions, without sacrificing the accuracy of your answers.

LETTER CHECKING

EXAMPLE 1

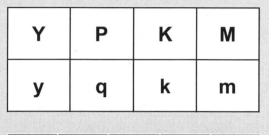

Question

How many letters match?

How to work it out

- There are four columns of letters. You will need to decide how many columns contain the same letter;

- Only choose pairs where the letter is the SAME as the letter in the same COLUMN;

- In the above example, you should notice that the 1st, 3rd and 4th column, all contain pairs of the same letter (Y and y; K and k; M and m);

- The 2nd column contains two different letters (P and q), and therefore does not match;

- The circle indicates what your chosen answer should be. Three of the columns contain matching letters, therefore 3 would be the correct answer.

Answer

3

Things to remember:

- Make sure you pay attention to the COLUMNS of letters;

- Watch out for letters that look the same (Q and o, P and q).

NUMBER DISTANCE

EXAMPLE 1

Question

What is the distant number?

How to work it out

- You will be given a set of numbers (like the above example). These numbers will appear in any order;

- You need to decide which number is the largest, and which is the smallest;

- You will then be left with the middle number. From that, you need to work out the difference between the middle number and the smallest number, and the middle number and the largest number.

Smallest number – 12

Middle number – 24

Largest number – 31

- So the difference between the smallest number and the middle number = 24 – 12 = 12.

- The difference between the largest number and the middle number = 31 – 24 = 7.

- Therefore, the distant number would be 12 (this is furthest away from the middle number).

Answer

12

Remember the following steps:

Step 1 = decide which number is the middle number.

Step 2 = now decide what the difference is between the middle number and the smallest number.

Step 3 = repeat step 2 again, but this time for the biggest number.

Step 4 = the number that is furthest away from the number in step 1, is the correct answer.

Note = your answer will ALWAYS be either the smallest number or the biggest number (NEVER the middle number).

ODD ONE OUT

EXAMPLE 1

Question

Which word is the odd one out?

How to work it out

- You will be given three words and you will need to determine which word is the odd one out;

- You need to consider how the words are linked (number of letters, rhyming, oppositions, synonyms etc);

- In the above example, you should notice that 'back' and 'lack' both rhyme. They have no clear link to the word 'cat'. Therefore the odd one out would be 'cat'.

Answer

Cat

ODD ONE OUT

EXAMPLE 2

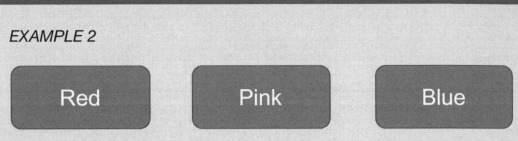

Red   **Pink**   **Blue**

Question

Which word is the odd one out?

How to work it out

- In this example, you might find it slightly trickier. All three words refer to a colour, so they are all linked in that way;

- However, you should notice that 'pink' and 'blue' both contain 4 letters, whereas 'red' only contains 3 letters. Therefore this makes 'red' the odd one out.

Answer

Red

Things to be considered:

- Anything can be the reason as to why the words are different. Look out for meanings, oppositions, rhyming words, syllables, number of letters, pronunciations.

SYMBOL ROTATION

EXAMPLE 1

F ⊓
Ш ⊓

Question

How many columns contain rotated symbols?

How to work it out

- Your task will be to take the two symbols from each column and determine whether the top shape **can** be rotated to match the bottom shape;

- So in example 1, if we take the first column, you will notice that the top shape can be rotated to match the bottom shape. The first shape highlighted (below) shows you what symbol you started off with; the second highlighted shape shows you that you **can** match the bottom shape by rotation, therefore this pair **does** match.

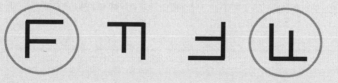

- If we take the second column, and look at the top symbol you should realise that no matter what way you rotate it, you will **not** be able to match the bottom shape (the bottom shape has been reflected as well as rotated), therefore it does not match;

- The highlighted shape (below) shows you the top shape of the column, but as you can see, it **cannot** make the bottom shape through rotation.

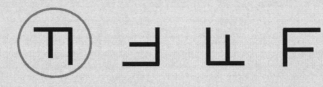

- Therefore, for this question only one pair matches.

Answer

1

Now that you have a clearer understanding of the five areas in which you will be assessed during your BARB Test, we have provided you with lots of sample questions to work through.

Work through each section, and then check your answers with our detailed explanations at the end of each section.

Please note, we have supplied you with more testing questions than what will appear in your actual test. We want to provide you with lots of sample questions in order to fully prepare you for your BARB Test.

Good luck.

BARB TEST – REASONING

TEST SECTION 1

> *You have 6 minutes in which to complete the 20 questions. Please note that the time limit placed on this exercise will not be the same as the one set during the real BARB Test.*

Question 1

Amelia is not as slim as Tina. Who is the slimmest?

Answer

Question 2

Michael is sadder than James. Who is less miserable?

Answer

Question 3

Peter is better at Maths than Elliott. Elliott is better at Maths than Robert. Who is the least able at Maths?

Answer

Question 4

Polly does more exercise than Ella. Who spends more time exercising?

Answer

Question 5

The red lorry is older than the blue lorry. Which lorry is the eldest?

Answer

Question 6

Mia spends 10% more on her food shopping compared with Dan, who spends 15% more than Josie. Who spends the least?

Answer

Question 7

Billy is more sensitive than Toby. Who is the least sensitive?

Answer

Question 8

Mark is not as lucky as Juliet. Who is less lucky?

Answer

Question 9

Ollie is shorter than Mike. Mike is 2 inches taller than David. Who is the tallest?

Answer

Question 10

Katie is brighter than Rachel. Who is duller?

Answer

Question 11

Haley is not as strong as Melanie. Who is the weakest?

Answer

Question 12

Richard works harder than Matthew. Who works the least hard?

Answer

Question 13

Kate is more confident than Natalie. Who is more timid?

Answer

Question 14

Imogen drinks quicker than Sarah. Who drinks the slowest?

Answer

Question 15

Gareth is in a higher class than Martin. Who is in the lower class?

Answer [ ]

Question 16

Felicity is more ambitious than Sandra. Who is more go-getting?

Answer [ ]

Question 17

Alecia finishes her homework before Lauren, but after Nancy. Who finishes their homework first?

Answer [ ]

Question 18

Lucy is less superstitious than Gemma. Who is more superstitious?

Answer [ ]

Question 19

Tom is less materialistic than his brother Jerry. Who is more acquisitive?

Answer [ ]

Question 20

Peter's holiday is more expensive than Wendy's. Whose holiday cost less?

Answer

BARB REASONING – TEST SECTION 1 ANSWERS

Q1. Tina

Q2. James

Q3. Robert

Q4. Polly

Q5. Red lorry

Q6. Josie

Q7. Toby

Q8. Mark

Q9. Mike

Q10. Rachel

Q11. Haley

Q12. Matthew

Q13. Natalie

Q14. Sarah

Q15. Martin

Q16. Felicity

Q17. Nancy

Q18. Gemma

Q19. Jerry

Q20. Wendy's

BARB TEST – REASONING

TEST SECTION 2

You have 6 minutes in which to complete the 20 questions. Please note that the time limit placed on this exercise will not be the same as the one set during the real BARB Test.

Question 1

Grace is quieter than Millie. Who is louder?

Answer

Question 2

Harriett is two dress sizes smaller than Tilly. Who is smaller?

Answer

Question 3

Elizabeth is less respectful than Courtney. Who is politer?

Answer

Question 4

Samuel is not as energetic as Ryan. Who is more energetic?

Answer

Question 5

Leah is less patient than Harrison. Who has the most patience?

Answer [   ]

Question 6

Ollie has a heavier workload than Dan. Who has less work?

Answer [   ]

Question 7

Jamie is twice as smart as Timothy, but half as smart as Marcus. Who is the smartest?

Answer [   ]

Question 8

Sammie has only a third of the amount of DVDs as Georgia. Who has the least amount of DVDs?

Answer [   ]

Question 9

Timmy is more argumentative than David. Who is more likely to get involved in a debate?

Answer [   ]

Question 10

Ronald finishes the race 2 minutes quicker than Rob, but 4 minutes after Jason. Who finishes the race last?

Answer

Question 11

Peter is older than Steve. Who was born first?

Answer

Question 12

Jack writes twice as many reports as Jamie. Jamie writes a third of the amount of Ellie. Who writes the least amount of reports?

Answer

Question 13

Freddie has twice the fortune of Danny. Who is wealthier?

Answer

Question 14

Mark is less religious than Keith. Religion is more important to who?

Answer

Question 15

Terry is angrier than George. Who is less angry?

Answer [   ]

Question 16

Michael needs more sleep than Cameron. Who needs less sleep?

Answer [   ]

Question 17

Danielle has more accidents than Sophie. Who is less accident-prone?

Answer [   ]

Question 18

Chris is quicker than Paul. Paul is slower than Jordan. Who is the slowest?

Answer [   ]

Question 19

Juliet lives 22 miles away from her work place. Anne's work place is 20 miles away from her home. Who has to travel the furthest to work?

Answer [   ]

Question 20

Melissa worked for 2 hours and ten minutes, whilst Ryan worked for 140 minutes. Who worked the shortest amount of time?

Answer [ ]

BARB REASONING – TEST SECTION 2 ANSWERS

Q1. Millie

Q2. Harriett

Q3. Courtney

Q4. Ryan

Q5. Harrison

Q6. Dan

Q7. Marcus

Q8. Sammie

Q9. Timmy

Q10. Rob

Q11. Peter

Q12. Jamie

Q13. Freddie

Q14. Keith

Q15. George

Q16. Cameron

Q17. Sophie

Q18. Paul

Q19. Juliet

Q20. Melissa

Now move on to the Letter Checking Test of the BARB Test.

BARB TEST – LETTER CHECKING

TEST SECTION 1

You have 6 minutes in which to complete the 20 questions. Please note that the time limit placed on this exercise will not be the same as the one set during the real BARB Test.

For the following questions, you should use the following question:

How many columns contain the same letters?
Please circle your answer.

Question 1

C	D	E	W
o	d	e	w

0	1	2	3	4

Question 2

S	E	B	N
s	a	p	m

0	1	2	3	4

Question 3

i	u	G	Y
L	V	g	y

0	1	2	3	4

Question 4

F	t	A	R
f	D	e	r

0	1	2	3	4

Question 5

C	h	j	k
c	H	J	K

0	1	2	3	4

Question 6

n	L	O	X
M	i	u	x

0	1	2	3	4

Question 7

j	T	d	f
J	t	P	T

0	1	2	3	4

Question 8

V	S	h	Q
v	S	H	p

0	1	2	3	4

Question 9

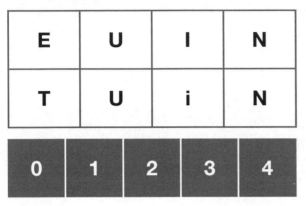

E	U	I	N
T	U	i	N

0	1	2	3	4

Question 10

o	K	Y	e
O	K	y	E

0	1	2	3	4

Question 11

g	H	E	r
G	h	e	R

0	1	2	3	4

Question 12

j	u	x	A
J	U	X	a

| 0 | 1 | 2 | 3 | 4 |

Question 13

u	R	E	w
V	T	A	M

| 0 | 1 | 2 | 3 | 4 |

Question 14

p	n	F	r
P	M	T	j

| 0 | 1 | 2 | 3 | 4 |

Question 15

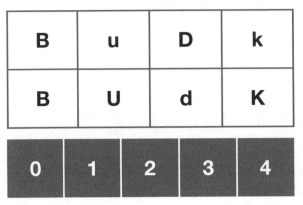

B	u	D	k
B	U	d	K

0	1	2	3	4

Question 16

Y	F	u	A
y	f	U	a

0	1	2	3	4

Question 17

p	A	S	e
P	a	s	E

0	1	2	3	4

Question 18

V	Z	B	g
v	z	B	p

0	1	2	3	4

Question 19

H	E	K	r
h	e	k	R

0	1	2	3	4

Question 20

g	R	j	C
P	T	L	o

0	1	2	3	4

BARB LETTER CHECKING – TEST SECTION 1 ANSWERS

Q1. 3

EXPLANATION = columns 2, 3 and 4 contain matching letters.

Q2. 1

EXPLANATION = column 1 contains matching letters.

Q3. 2

EXPLANATION = columns 3 and 4 contain matching letters.

Q4. 2

EXPLANATION = columns 1 and 4 contain matching letters.

Q5. 4

EXPLANATION = all four columns contain matching letters.

Q6. 1

EXPLANATION = column 4 contains matching letters.

Q7. 2

EXPLANATION = columns 1 and 2 contain matching letters.

Q8. 3

EXPLANATION = columns 1, 2 and 3 contain matching letters.

Q9. 3

EXPLANATION = columns 2, 3 and 4 contain matching letters.

Q10. 4

EXPLANATION = all four columns contain matching letters.

Q11. 4

EXPLANATION = all four columns contain matching letters.

Q12. 4

EXPLANATION = all four columns contain matching letters.

Q13. 0

EXPLANATION = no columns contain matching letters.

Q14. 1

EXPLANATION = column 1 contains matching letters.

Q15. 4

EXPLANATION = all four columns contain matching letters.

Q16. 4

EXPLANATION = all four columns contain matching letters.

Q17. 4

EXPLANATION = all four columns contain matching letters.

Q18. 3

EXPLANATION = columns 1, 2 and 3 contain matching letters.

Q19. 4

EXPLANATION = all four columns contain matching letters.

Q20. 0

EXPLANATION = no columns contain matching letters.

BARB TEST – LETTER CHECKING

TEST SECTION 2

You have 6 minutes in which to complete the 20 questions. Please note that the time limit placed on this exercise will not be the same as the one set during the real BARB Test.

For the following questions, you should use the following question:

How many columns contain the same letters?
Please circle your answer.

Question 1

u	i	a	x
V	L	A	X

0	1	2	3	4

Question 2

p	c	o	k
P	C	O	K

0	1	2	3	4

Question 3

y	j	B	r
Y	G	P	A

0	1	2	3	4

Question 4

b	h	E	d
p	H	a	B

0	1	2	3	4

Question 5

u	o	i	l
v	o	i	l

0	1	2	3	4

Question 6

h	b	w	a
H	d	W	A

0	1	2	3	4

Question 7

E	h	r	D
e	H	R	d

0	1	2	3	4

Question 8

K	o	b	a
k	o	D	A

0	1	2	3	4

Question 9

y	g	f	t
Y	G	F	T

0	1	2	3	4

Question 10

a	j	p	o
E	J	p	o

0	1	2	3	4

Question 11

E	A	x	u
e	a	p	o

0	1	2	3	4

Question 12

y	j	t	f
j	G	F	T

0	1	2	3	4

Question 13

i	D	H	a
L	b	H	e

0	1	2	3	4

Question 14

u	B	i	s
a	a	L	p

0	1	2	3	4

Question 15

y	j	L	f
j	K	i	T

0	1	2	3	4

Question 16

n	m	w	G
N	W	W	G

0	1	2	3	4

Question 17

u	E	s	f
E	a	L	t

0	1	2	3	4

Question 18

j	t	e	z
J	f	u	Z

0	1	2	3	4

Question 19

A	e	m	d
a	i	n	f

0	1	2	3	4

Question 20

T	D	j	o
T	D	j	e

0	1	2	3	4

BARB LETTER CHECKING – TEST SECTION 2 ANSWERS

Q1. 2

EXPLANATION = columns 3 and 4 contain matching letters.

Q2. 4

EXPLANATION = all four columns contain matching letters.

Q3. 1

EXPLANATION = column 1 contains matching letters.

Q4. 1

EXPLANATION = column 2 contains matching letters.

Q5. 3

EXPLANATION = columns 2, 3 and 4 contain matching letters.

Q6. 3

EXPLANATION = columns 1, 3 and 4 contain matching letters.

Q7. 4

EXPLANATION = all four columns contain matching letters.

Q8. 3

EXPLANATION = columns 1, 2 and 4 contain matching letters.

Q9. 4

EXPLANATION = all four columns contain matching letters.

Q10. 3

EXPLANATION = columns 2, 3 and 4 contain matching letters.

Q11. 2

EXPLANATION = columns 1 and 2 contain matching letters.

Q12. 0

EXPLANATION = no columns contain matching letters.

Q13. 1

EXPLANATION = column 3 contains matching letters.

Q14. 0

EXPLANATION = no columns contain matching letters.

Q15. 0

EXPLANATION = no columns contain matching letters.

Q16. 3

EXPLANATION = columns 1, 3 and 4 contain matching letters.

Q17. 0

EXPLANATION = no columns contain matching letters.

Q18. 2

EXPLANATION = columns 1 and 4 contain matching letters.

Q19. 1

EXPLANATION = column 1 contains matching letters.

Q20. 3

EXPLANATION = columns 1, 2 and 3 contain matching letters.

Now move on to the Number Distance Test of the BARB Test.

BARB TEST – NUMBER DISTANCE

TEST SECTION 1

You have 8 minutes in which to complete the 20 questions. Please note that the time limit placed on this exercise will not be the same as the one set during the real BARB Test.

For the following 20 questions, you should use the following question:

Decide which number is the smallest, and which is the biggest, and work out which of these numbers is the furthest away from the middle number.

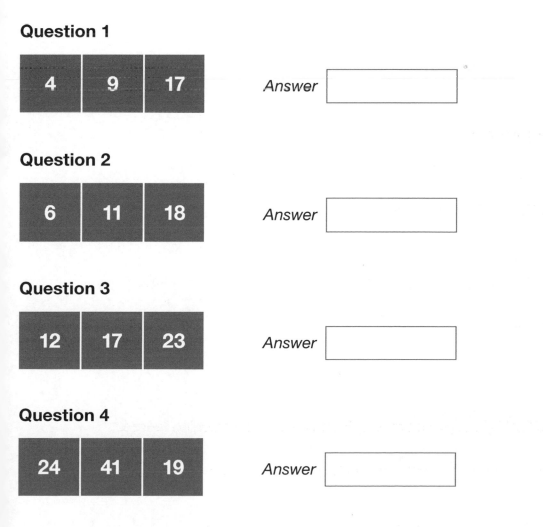

Question 1

4	9	17

Answer [ ]

Question 2

6	11	18

Answer [ ]

Question 3

12	17	23

Answer [ ]

Question 4

24	41	19

Answer [ ]

Question 5

| 63 | 13 | 29 |

Answer

Question 6

| 27 | 9 | 33 |

Answer

Question 7

| 53 | 22 | 31 |

Answer

Question 8

| 67 | 56 | 41 |

Answer

Question 9

| 68 | 1 | 34 |

Answer

Question 10

| 55 | 62 | 78 |

Answer

Question 11

| 98 | 1 | 47 |

Answer [   ]

Question 12

| 87 | 83 | 90 |

Answer [   ]

Question 13

| 103 | 77 | 81 |

Answer [   ]

Question 14

| 121 | 156 | 203 |

Answer [   ]

Question 15

| 321 | 407 | 285 |

Answer [   ]

Question 16

| 324 | 387 | 358 |

Answer [   ]

Question 17

| 208 | 196 | 275 |

Answer

Question 18

| 199 | 401 | 302 |

Answer

Question 19

| 553 | 297 | 217 |

Answer

Question 20

| 431 | 1 | 367 |

Answer

BARB NUMBER DISTANCE – TEST SECTION 1 ANSWERS

Q1. 17

Step 1 = smallest number = 4

Step 2 = biggest number = 17

Step 3 = 9 – 4 = 5

$\quad$ = 17 – 9 = 8

Therefore, 17 is the distant number.

Q2. 18

Step 1 = smallest number = 6

Step 2 = biggest number = 18

Step 3 = 11 – 6 = 5

$\quad$ = 18 – 11 = 7

Therefore, 18 is the distant number.

Q3. 23

Step 1 = smallest number = 12

Step 2 = biggest number = 23

Step 3 = 17 – 12 = 5

$\quad$ = 23 – 17 = 6

Therefore, 23 is the distant number.

Q4. 41

Step 1 = smallest number = 19

Step 2 = biggest number = 41

Step 3 = 24 − 19 = 5

$\qquad$ = 41 − 24 = 17

Therefore, 41 is the distant number.

Q5. 63

Step 1 = smallest number = 13

Step 2 = biggest number = 63

Step 3 = 29 − 13 = 16

$\qquad$ = 63 − 29 = 34

Therefore, 63 is the distant number.

Q6. 9

Step 1 = smallest number = 9

Step 2 = biggest number = 33

Step 3 = 27 − 9 = 18

$\qquad$ = 33 − 27 = 6

Therefore, 9 is the distant number.

Q7. 53

Step 1 = smallest number = 22

Step 2 = biggest number = 53

Step 3 = 31 − 22 = 9

$\qquad$ = 53 − 31 = 22

Therefore, 53 is the distant number.

Q8. 41

Step 1 = smallest number = 41

Step 2 = biggest number = 67

Step 3 = 56 – 41 = 15

     = 67 – 56 = 11

Therefore, 41 is the distant number.

Q9. 68

Step 1 = smallest number = 1

Step 2 = biggest number = 68

Step 3 = 34 – 1 = 33

     = 68 – 34 = 34

Therefore, 68 is the distant number.

Q10. 78

Step 1 = smallest number = 55

Step 2 = biggest number = 78

Step 3 = 62 – 55 = 7

     = 78 – 62 = 16

Therefore, 78 is the distant number.

Q11. 98

Step 1 = smallest number = 1

Step 2 = biggest number = 98

Step 3 = 47 – 1 = 46

     = 98 – 47 = 51

Therefore, 98 is the distant number.

Q12. 83

Step 1 = smallest number = 83

Step 2 = biggest number = 90

Step 3 = 87 – 83 = 4

$\qquad$ = 90 – 87 = 3

Therefore, 83 is the distant number.

Q13. 103

Step 1 = smallest number = 77

Step 2 = biggest number = 103

Step 3 = 81 – 77 = 4

$\qquad$ = 103 – 81 = 22

Therefore, 103 is the distant number.

Q14. 203

Step 1 = smallest number =121

Step 2 = biggest number = 203

Step 3 = 156 – 121 = 35

$\qquad$ = 203 – 156 = 47

Therefore, 203 is the distant number.

Q15. 407

Step 1 = smallest number = 285

Step 2 = biggest number = 407

Step 3 = 321 – 285 = 36

$\qquad$ = 407 – 321 = 86

Therefore, 407 is the distant number.

Q16. 324

Step 1 = smallest number = 324

Step 2 = biggest number = 387

Step 3 = 358 − 324 = 34

$\qquad$ = 387 − 358 = 29

Therefore, 324 is the distant number.

Q17. 275

Step 1 = smallest number = 196

Step 2 = biggest number = 275

Step 3 = 208 − 196 = 12

$\qquad$ = 275 − 208 = 67

Therefore, 275 is the distant number.

Q18. 199

Step 1 = smallest number = 199

Step 2 = biggest number = 401

Step 3 = 302 − 199 = 103

$\qquad$ = 401 − 302 = 99

Therefore, 199 is the distant number.

Q19. 553

Step 1 = smallest number = 217

Step 2 = biggest number = 553

Step 3 = 297 − 217 = 80

$\qquad$ = 553 − 297 = 256

Therefore, 553 is the distant number.

Q20. 1

Step 1 = smallest number = 1

Step 2 = biggest number = 431

Step 3 = 367 − 1 = 366

        = 431 − 367 = 64

Therefore, 1 is the distant number.

BARB TEST – NUMBER DISTANCE

TEST SECTION 2

You have 8 minutes in which to complete the 20 questions. Please note that the time limit placed on this exercise will not be the same as the one set during the real BARB Test.

For the following 20 questions, you should use the following question:

Decide which number is the smallest, and which is the biggest, and work out which of these numbers is the furthest away from the middle number.

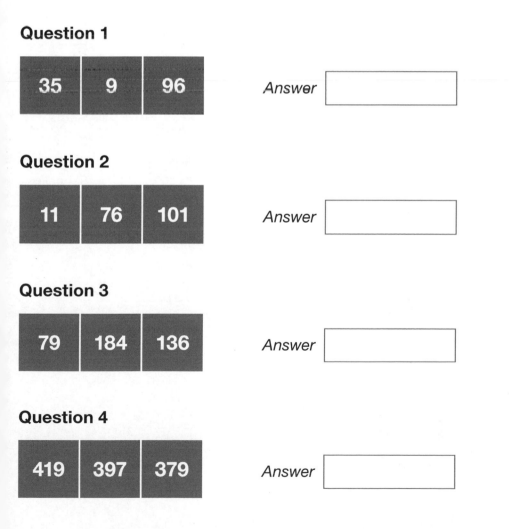

Question 1

| 35 | 9 | 96 |

Answer [ ]

Question 2

| 11 | 76 | 101 |

Answer [ ]

Question 3

| 79 | 184 | 136 |

Answer [ ]

Question 4

| 419 | 397 | 379 |

Answer [ ]

Question 5

| 372 | 363 | 359 |

Answer [   ]

Question 6

| 753 | 634 | 953 |

Answer [   ]

Question 7

| 345 | 363 | 314 |

Answer [   ]

Question 8

| 147 | 75 | 153 |

Answer [   ]

Question 9

| 136 | 216 | 175 |

Answer [   ]

Question 10

| 1 | 100 | 49 |

Answer [   ]

Question 11

| 755 | 346 | 586 |

Answer

Question 12

| 245 | 363 | 585 |

Answer

Question 13

| 64 | 46 | 85 |

Answer

Question 14

| 647 | 618 | 689 |

Answer

Question 15

| 12 | 37 | 63 |

Answer

Question 16

| 24 | 87 | 58 |

Answer

Question 17

| 20 | 96 | 75 |

Answer

Question 18

| 413 | 401 | 396 |

Answer

Question 19

| 53 | 97 | 21 |

Answer

Question 20

| 75 | 1 | 96 |

Answer

BARB NUMBER DISTANCE – TEST SECTION 2 ANSWERS

Q1. 96

Step 1 = smallest number = 9

Step 2 = biggest number = 96

Step 3 = 35 – 9 = 26

$\quad\quad$ = 96 – 35 = 61

Therefore, 96 is the distant number.

Q2. 11

Step 1 = smallest number = 11

Step 2 = biggest number = 101

Step 3 = 76 – 11 = 65

$\quad\quad$ = 101 – 76 = 25

Therefore, 11 is the distant number.

Q3. 79

Step 1 = smallest number = 79

Step 2 = biggest number = 184

Step 3 = 136 – 79 = 57

$\quad\quad$ = 184 – 136 = 48

Therefore, 79 is the distant number.

Q4. 419

Step 1 = smallest number = 379

Step 2 = biggest number = 419

Step 3 = 397 − 379 = 18

    = 419 − 397 = 22

Therefore, 419 is the distant number.

Q5. 372

Step 1 = smallest number = 359

Step 2 = biggest number = 372

Step 3 = 363 − 359 = 4

    = 372 − 363 = 9

Therefore, 372 is the distant number.

Q6. 953

Step 1 = smallest number = 634

Step 2 = biggest number = 953

Step 3 = 753 − 634 = 119

    = 953 − 753 = 200

Therefore, 953 is the distant number.

Q7. 314

Step 1 = smallest number = 314

Step 2 = biggest number = 363

Step 3 = 345 − 314 = 31

    = 363 − 345 = 18

Therefore, 314 is the distant number.

Q8. 75

Step 1 = smallest number = 75

Step 2 = biggest number = 153

Step 3 = 147 – 75 = 72

      = 153 – 147 = 6

Therefore, 75 is the distant number.

Q9. 216

Step 1 = smallest number = 136

Step 2 = biggest number = 216

Step 3 = 175 – 136 = 39

      = 216 – 175 = 41

Therefore, 216 is the distant number.

Q10. 100

Step 1 = smallest number = 1

Step 2 = biggest number = 100

Step 3 = 49 – 1 = 48

      = 100 – 49 = 51

Therefore, 100 is the distant number.

Q11. 346

Step 1 = smallest number = 346

Step 2 = biggest number = 755

Step 3 = 586 – 346 = 240

      = 755 – 586 = 169

Therefore, 346 is the distant number.

Q12. 585

Step 1 = smallest number = 245

Step 2 = biggest number = 585

Step 3 = 363 − 245 = 118

$\qquad$ = 585 − 363 = 222

Therefore, 585 is the distant number.

Q13. 85

Step 1 = smallest number = 46

Step 2 = biggest number = 85

Step 3 = 64 − 46 = 18

$\qquad$ = 85 − 64 = 21

Therefore, 85 is the distant number.

Q14. 689

Step 1 = smallest number = 618

Step 2 = biggest number = 689

Step 3 = 647 − 618 = 29

$\qquad$ = 689 − 647 = 42

Therefore, 689 is the distant number.

Q15. 63

Step 1 = smallest number = 12

Step 2 = biggest number = 63

Step 3 = 37 − 12 = 25

$\qquad$ = 63 − 37 = 26

Therefore, 63 is the distant number.

Q16. 24

Step 1 = smallest number = 24

Step 2 = biggest number = 87

Step 3 = 58 − 24 = 34

$\qquad$ = 87 − 58 = 29

Therefore, 24 is the distant number.

Q17. 20

Step 1 = smallest number = 20

Step 2 = biggest number = 96

Step 3 = 75 − 20 = 55

$\qquad$ = 96 − 75 = 21

Therefore, 20 is the distant number.

Q18. 413

Step 1 = smallest number = 396

Step 2 = biggest number = 413

Step 3 = 401 − 396 = 5

$\qquad$ = 413 − 401 = 12

Therefore, 413 is the distant number.

Q19. 97

Step 1 = smallest number = 21

Step 2 = biggest number = 97

Step 3 = 53 − 21 = 32

$\qquad$ = 97 − 53 = 44

Therefore, 97 is the distant number.

Q20. 1

Step 1 = smallest number = 1

Step 2 = biggest number = 96

Step 3 = 75 − 1 = 74

        = 96 − 75 = 21

Therefore, 1 is the distant number.

Now move on to the Odd One Out section of the BARB Test.

BARB TEST – ODD ONE OUT

TEST SECTION 1

You have 3 minutes in which to complete the 20 questions. Please note that the time limit placed on this exercise will not be the same as the one set during the real BARB Test.

For the following 20 questions, use the following question:

Which word is the odd one out?
Please circle which word is the odd one out.

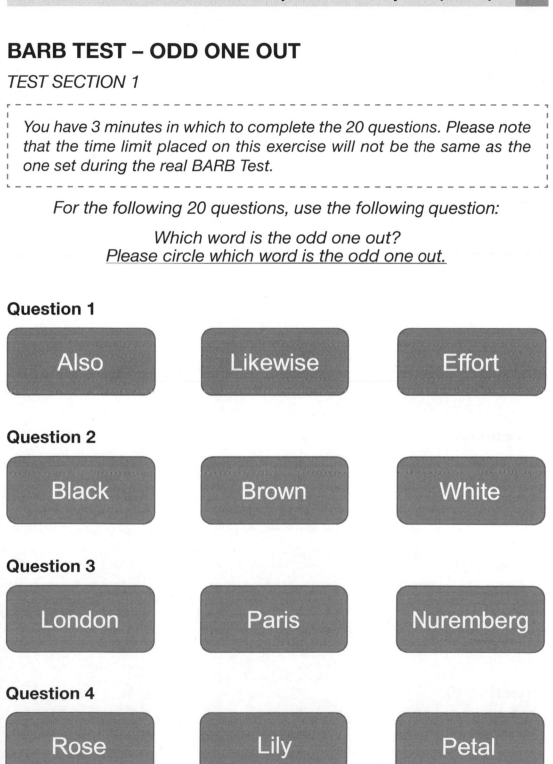

Question 1

Also   Likewise   Effort

Question 2

Black   Brown   White

Question 3

London   Paris   Nuremberg

Question 4

Rose   Lily   Petal

Question 5

Dull	Bright	Exciting

Question 6

Quiet	Bang	Silent

Question 7

Boat	Ship	Train

Question 8

Arouse	Dangerous	Provoke

Question 9

Under	Deep	Over

Question 10

Apple	Melon	Carrot

Question 11

Track	Grass	Train

Question 12

Past	Future	Anticipate

Question 13

Closed	Ended	Open

Question 14

Anger	Timid	Wrath

Question 15

Allotment	Soil	Stones

Question 16

Funeral	Divorced	Married

Question 17

| Right | Temper | Wrong |

Question 18

| Robust | Frail | Glass |

Question 19

| New | Dead | Original |

Question 20

| Cluttered | Wretched | Organised |

BARB ODD ONE OUT – TEST SECTION 1 ANSWERS

Q1. Effort

EXPLANATION = 'also' and 'likewise' both mean *similarly*; i.e. *in a similar manner.* Therefore the odd one out would be 'effort'.

Q2. Brown

EXPLANATION = 'brown' is the odd one out because, and despite all the words referring to colours, 'black' is the opposite to 'white'.

Q3. Nuremberg

EXPLANATION = 'Nuremberg' is the odd one out because 'Paris' and 'London' are both capital cities, whereas Nuremberg is just a city; not a capital city.

Q4. Petal

EXPLANATION = 'petal' is the odd one out because 'rose' and 'lily' are both *types* of flowers, whereas 'petal' is *part* of a flower.

Q5. Exciting

EXPLANATION = 'exciting' is the odd one out because 'dull' is the opposite to 'bright', and therefore the words can be linked.

Q6. Bang

EXPLANATION = 'bang' is the odd one out because 'quiet' and 'silent' both carry the same meaning, whereas 'bang' has the opposite meaning.

Q7. Train

EXPLANATION = 'train' is the odd one out because both 'ship' and 'boat' are types of transport across water.

Q8. Dangerous

EXPLANATION = 'dangerous' is the odd one out because 'provoke' and 'arouse' refer to stimulating or inducing emotions.

Q9. Deep

EXPLANATION = 'deep' is the odd one out because 'under' and 'over' are the opposites of one another. 'Deep' has no clear link to either of these words.

Q10. Carrot

EXPLANATION = 'carrot' is the odd one out because 'melon' and 'apple' are types of *fruit*, whereas 'carrot' is a type of *vegetable*.

Q11. Grass

EXPLANATION = 'grass' is the odd one out because both 'train' and 'track' refer to parts of a railway, whereas 'grass' has no clear link to either of these words.

Q12. Anticipate

EXPLANATION = 'anticipate' is the odd one out because 'past' is the opposite to 'future' and therefore the words can be linked, whereas 'anticipate' has no clear link to either of these words.

Q13. Ended

EXPLANATION = 'open' and 'closed' are two words that can be linked; they are the opposites of one another. 'Ended' has no clear link to either of these words.

Q14. Timid

EXPLANATION = 'timid' is the odd one out because 'anger' and 'wrath' carry similar meanings. Both of these words refer to rage and fury. 'Timid' has a completely different meaning and therefore cannot be linked to either of these words.

Q15. Stones

EXPLANATION = 'stones' is the odd one out because 'allotment' and 'soil' refer to the contents found in an allotment. An allotment will contain soil, and therefore the words have a clear connection. 'Stones' does not share this connection, and is therefore the odd one out.

Q16. Funeral

EXPLANATION = 'funeral' is the odd one out because 'married' and 'divorced' are the opposite in meaning, and therefore share a link between them. 'Funeral' does not link to either of these words.

Q17. Temper

EXPLANATION = 'temper' is the odd one out because 'right' and 'wrong' are the opposite in meaning, and therefore share a link. 'Temper' does not link to either of these words.

Q18. Glass

EXPLANATION = 'glass' is the odd one out because 'robust' and 'frail' are opposite in meaning, and therefore share a link. 'Glass' does not share a similar link and is therefore the odd one out.

Q19. Dead

EXPLANATION 'dead' is the odd one out because 'new' and 'original' both mean similar things. 'Dead' does not link to either of these words.

Q20. Wretched

EXPLANATION = 'wretched' is the odd one out because 'cluttered' is the opposite to 'organised', and therefore shares a link between them. 'Wretched' does not link to either of these words.

BARB TEST – ODD ONE OUT

TEST SECTION 2

You have 3 minutes in which to complete the 20 questions. Please note that the time limit placed on this exercise will not be the same as the one set during the real BARB Test.

For the following 20 questions, use the following question:

Which word is the odd one out?
Please circle which word is the odd one out.

Question 1

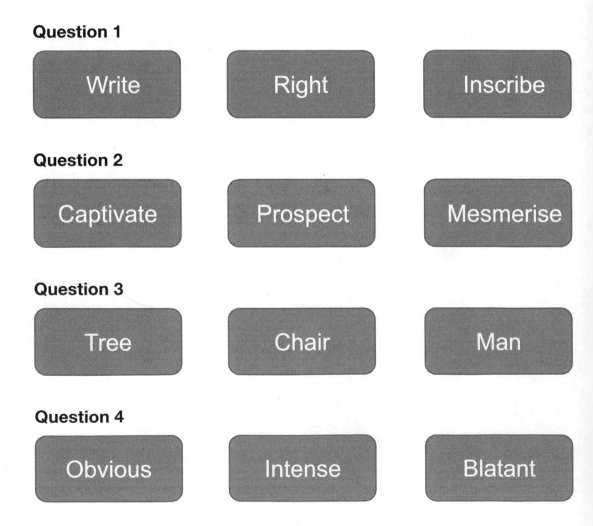

| Write | Right | Inscribe |

Question 2

| Captivate | Prospect | Mesmerise |

Question 3

| Tree | Chair | Man |

Question 4

| Obvious | Intense | Blatant |

Question 5

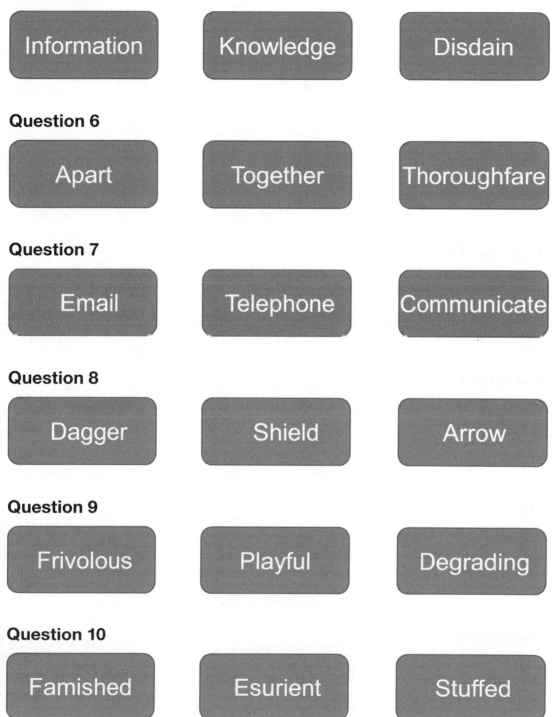

Information   Knowledge   Disdain

Question 6

Apart   Together   Thoroughfare

Question 7

Email   Telephone   Communicate

Question 8

Dagger   Shield   Arrow

Question 9

Frivolous   Playful   Degrading

Question 10

Famished   Esurient   Stuffed

Question 11

Jaded   Enervated   Jovial

Question 12

Chare   Bench   Sofa

Question 13

Illusion   Fantasy   Time

Question 14

Veracity   Apocryphal   Mythical

Question 15

Congenial   Insolent   Affable

Question 16

Hope   Nihilism   Optimism

Question 17

Narcissistic	Conceited	Indifferent

Question 18

Love	Hate	Dead

Question 19

Futile	Engross	Pointless

Question 20

Apprehensive	Problematic	Easy

BARB ODD ONE OUT – TEST SECTION 2 ANSWERS

Q1. Right

EXPLANATION = 'right' is the odd one out because 'write' and 'inscribe' are both words used to illustrate *writing something.* 'Right' is a word used to indicate whether something is *correct.*

Q2. Prospect

EXPLANATION = 'prospect' is the odd one out because both 'captivate' and 'mesmerise' are words used to describe something that holds interest and attraction.

Q3. Chair

EXPLANATION = 'chair' is the odd one out because both 'tree' and 'man' refer to living things, whereas 'chair' is an inanimate object.

Q4. Intense

EXPLANATION = 'intense' is the odd one out because both 'obvious' and 'blatant' are words that can be used to describe something that is clear or apparent, whereas 'intense' is a word used to describe strong feelings or extreme force.

Q5. Disdain

EXPLANATION = 'disdain' is the odd one out because both 'information' and 'knowledge' refer to types of data and information sources that you can collate to improve your intellectual ability. 'Disdain' is a word used to describe something or someone that is unworthy.

Q6. Thoroughfare

EXPLANATION = 'thoroughfare' is the odd one out because both 'apart' and 'together' are words that can be linked; they are words that are opposites of one another. Whereas 'thoroughfare' is a word used to describe a road or route between two places.

Q7. Communicate

EXPLANATION = 'communicate' is the odd one out because both of the other words refer to a *type* of communication, whereas 'communicate' is the word used to describe what both of these words are essentially doing.

Q8. Shield

EXPLANATION = 'shield' is the odd one out because both 'dagger' and 'arrow' are *types of weaponry,* whereas a 'shield' is a *means of protection*.

Q9. Degrading

EXPLANATION = 'degrading' is the odd one out because the other words refer to types of behaviour that are carefree and don't have any serious value. 'Degrading' is a word used to indicate a loss of self-respect i.e. humiliation.

Q10. Stuffed

EXPLANATION – 'stuffed' is the odd one out because both 'famished' and 'esurient' are words used to describe hunger. 'Stuffed' is the complete opposite to both of these words.

Q11. Jovial

EXPLANATION = 'jovial' is the odd one out because both 'jaded' and 'enervated' are words used to describe tiredness and exhaustion. Whereas, 'jovial' is a word used to describe cheerfulness and happiness.

Q12. Chare

EXPLANATION = 'chare' is the odd one out because both 'sofa' and 'bench' are objects in which you can sit on. A *chare* refers to a small medieval street or alley.

Q13. Time

EXPLANATION = 'time' is the odd one out because both 'illusion' and 'fantasy' refer to types of imaginary beliefs. 'Time' has no clear relationship with either of these words, and is therefore the odd one out.

Q14. Veracity

EXPLANATION = 'veracity' is the odd one out because both 'apocryphal' and 'mythical' are words used to illustrate doubtful authenticity; it is in other words, fictitious. 'Veracity' is a word used to illustrate truth and logic.

Q15. Insolent

EXPLANATION = 'insolent' is the odd one out because both 'congenial' and 'affable' are words used to describe someone who is friendly and pleasant. 'Insolent' is a word used to describe someone who is rude and arrogant.

Q16. Nihilism

EXPLANATION = 'nihilism' is the odd one out because both 'hope' and 'optimism' refer to faith and a positive outlook. Whereas 'nihilism' is a word used to reject all religious or moral principles; often believing that life is meaningless.

Q17. Indifferent

EXPLANATION = 'indifferent' is the odd one out because both 'narcissistic' and 'conceited' are words used to describe someone who is egotistical and vain. 'Indifferent' is a word used to describe someone who shows no interest or sympathy i.e. uncaring.

Q18. Dead

EXPLANATION = 'dead' is the odd one out because both 'love' and 'hate' can be closely linked; both words can be used to describe a person's relationship with something or someone. 'Dead' shows no clear connection with either of these words.

Q19. Engross

EXPLANATION = 'engross' is the odd one out because both 'futile' and 'pointless' are words that can be used to highlight the inability to produce useful results, i.e. it is pointless. 'Engross' is a word that can be used to show someone absorbing the attention or interest of something or someone.

Q20. Apprehensive

EXPLANATION = 'apprehensive' is the odd one out because 'problematic' is the opposite of 'easy', and therefore the words show a certain connection. 'Apprehensive' is a feeling of anxiety and fear, and therefore shows no clear connection with the other words.

Now move on to the Symbol Rotation Test of the BARB Test.

BARB TEST – SYMBOL ROTATION

TEST SECTION 1

You have 6 minutes in which to complete the 20 questions. Please note that the time limit placed on this exercise will not be the same as the one set during the real BARB Test.

Identify how many pairs of letters or symbols match in each sequence. <u>Please circle your answer.</u>

Question 1

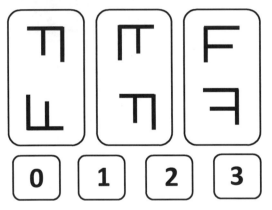

Question 2

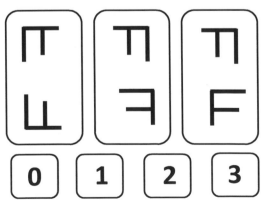

Question 3

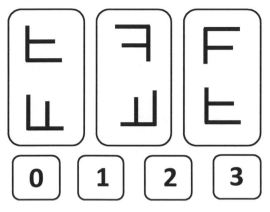

| 0 | 1 | 2 | 3 |

Question 4

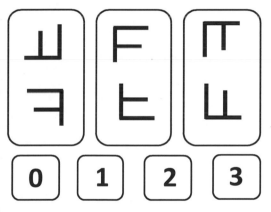

| 0 | 1 | 2 | 3 |

Question 5

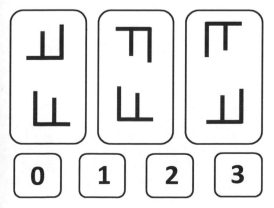

| 0 | 1 | 2 | 3 |

Question 6

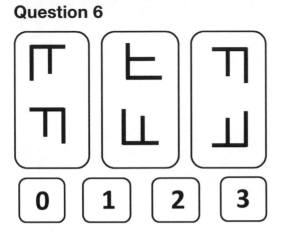

Question 7

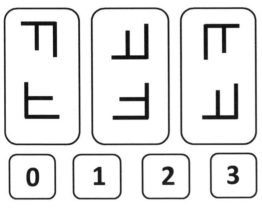

Question 8

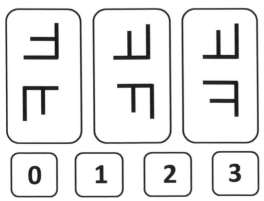

Question 9

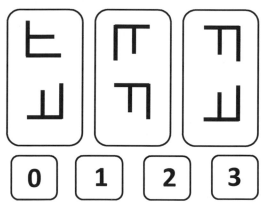

Question 10

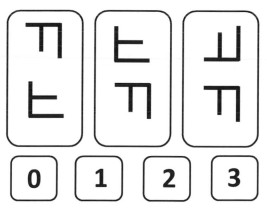

Question 11

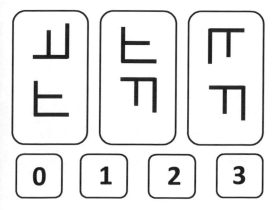

Question 12

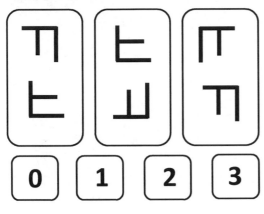

Question 13

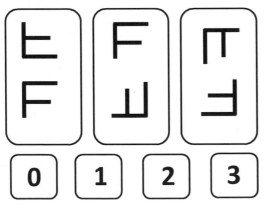

Question 14

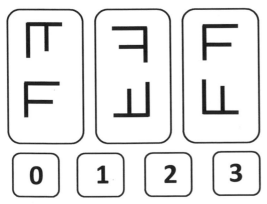

Question 15

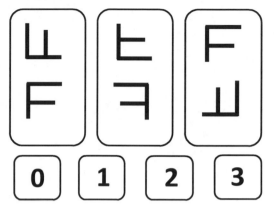

Question 16

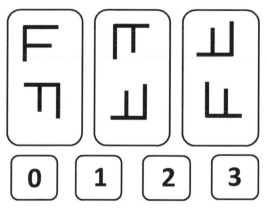

Question 17

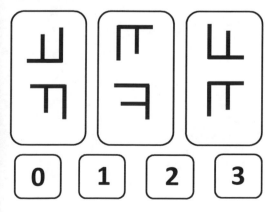

Question 18

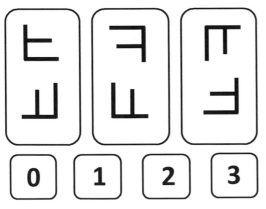

0   1   2   3

Question 19

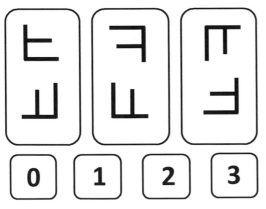

0   1   2   3

Question 20

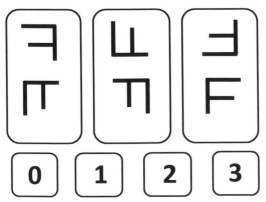

0   1   2   3

BARB SYMBOL ROTATION – TEST SECTION 1 ANSWERS

Q1. 1

Q2. 1

Q3. 1

Q4. 1

Q5. 2

Q6. 0

Q7. 1

Q8. 1

Q9. 1

Q10. 0

Q11. 1

Q12. 1

Q13. 0

Q14. 2

Q15. 2

Q16. 2

Q17. 1

Q18. 3

Q19. 1

Q20. 3

BARB TEST – SYMBOL ROTATION

TEST SECTION 2

You have 6 minutes in which to complete the 20 questions. Please note that the time limit placed on this exercise will not be the same as the one set during the real BARB Test.

Identify how many pairs of letters or symbols match in each sequence. <u>Please circle your answer.</u>

Question 1

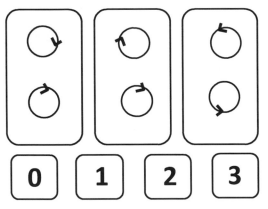

Question 2

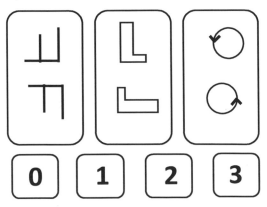

Question 3

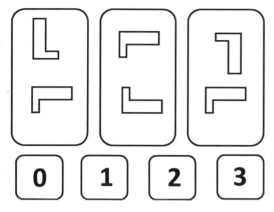

Question 4

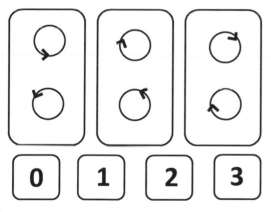

Question 5

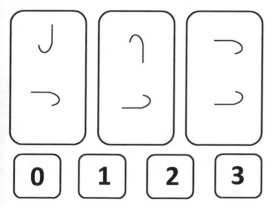

Question 6

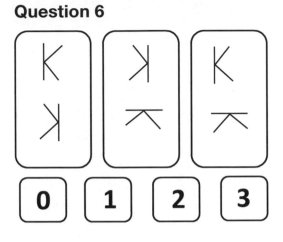

Question 7

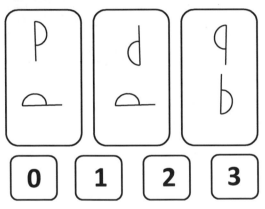

Question 8

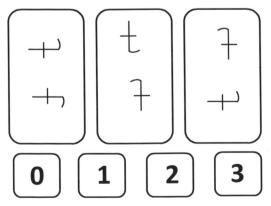

Question 9

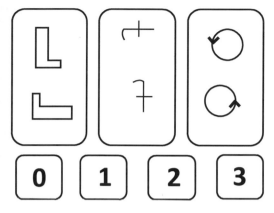

| 0 | 1 | 2 | 3 |

Question 10

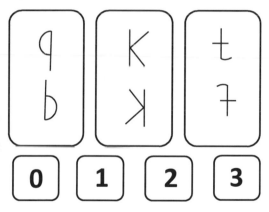

| 0 | 1 | 2 | 3 |

Question 11

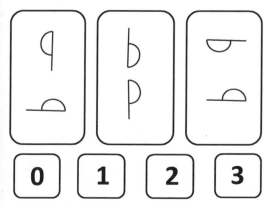

| 0 | 1 | 2 | 3 |

Question 12

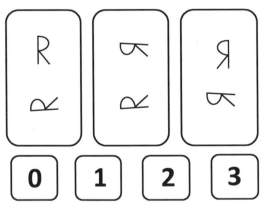

| 0 | 1 | 2 | 3 |

Question 13

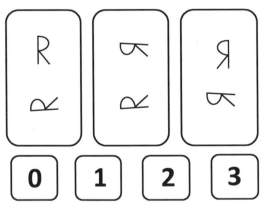

| 0 | 1 | 2 | 3 |

Question 14

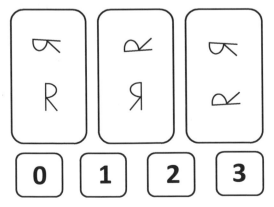

| 0 | 1 | 2 | 3 |

Question 15

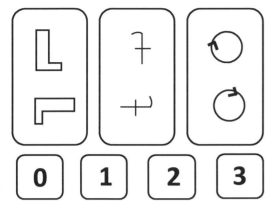

0 **1** **2** **3**

Question 16

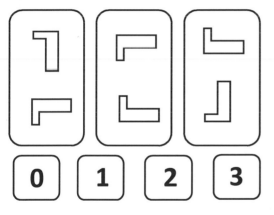

0 **1** **2** **3**

Question 17

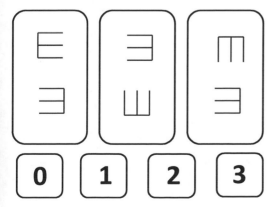

0 **1** **2** **3**

Question 18

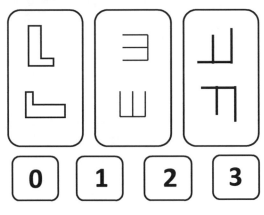

Question 19

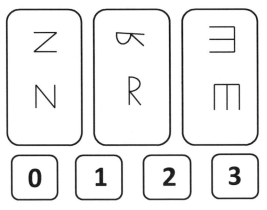

Question 20

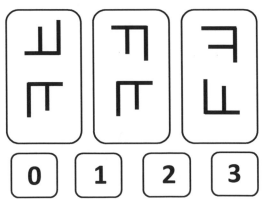

BARB SYMBOL ROTATION – TEST SECTION 2 ANSWERS

Q1. 3

Q2. 1

Q3. 2

Q4. 2

Q5. 2

Q6. 3

Q7. 3

Q8. 2

Q9. 2

Q10. 3

Q11. 2

Q12. 3

Q13. 2

Q14. 0

Q15. 3

Q16. 2

Q17. 3

Q18. 1

Q19. 2

Q20. 1

You have now completed your BARB Test.

The Royal Navy Recruiting Test (RT)

WHAT IS THE ROYAL NAVY RECRUITING TEST?

The Royal Navy Recruiting Test (RT) will test whether you have the skills needed to join the Royal Navy. These tests are a reflection of how well you are likely to perform in a specific role within the Royal Navy. It does not matter what qualifications you have, you will still be required to sit the RT, and your results will go towards determining your suitability for the Armed Forces. Your performance in the RT will demonstrate your ability to cope with the technical and academic requirements needed to join the Royal Navy.

WHO NEEDS TO TAKE THE ROYAL NAVY RECRUITING TEST?

If you are applying to join the Royal Navy at any position or level, you will be required to complete the Recruiting Test.

WHY DO I NEED TO BE ASSESSED?

The main purpose of the Royal Navy Recruiting Test is to establish how effective you are at figuring out problems, assess your English and Mathematical ability, and determine whether or not you are able to understand basic mechanical concepts.

Psychometric tests are a useful way of deciphering a person's level of intellectual, critical and technical ability. These tests evaluate a candidate's performance in terms of how well they can cope with the technical and demanding nature of the Naval Service.

WHAT DOES THE ROYAL NAVY RECRUITING TEST CONSIST OF?

The Royal Navy Recruiting Test covers the following four areas:

- *A Reasoning Test (30 questions to be completed in 9 minutes);*
- *A Verbal Ability Test (30 questions to be completed in 9 minutes);*
- *A Numeracy Test (30 questions to be completed in 16 minutes);*

- *A Mechanical Comprehension Test (30 questions to be completed in 10 minutes).*

The tests are usually carried out at the Armed Forces Careers Office and will be taken under strict timed conditions. Details of the time restrictions and number of questions per exercise will be provided in your recruitment literature. Your recruitment literature is key! Make sure that you take the time to thoroughly read through the whole booklet so you are fully aware of the expectations of your assessment. The pass mark for the Royal Navy Recruiting Test will depend on the technical ability level required for the post for which you are applying; although a pass mark of 50% is normally sufficient for the majority of branches.

TIPS FOR PASSING THE ROYAL NAVY RECRUITING TEST

- Undergo as much practice as you can. The more practice you undergo, the more competent you will become, thus improving your overall scores and performance;

- Focus on practising the questions you struggle with first. Tackling the questions that you find most difficult will ensure that your weaker areas have been revised and conquered;

- *Reasoning Test* – the more question *types* you practice, the better prepared you will feel. The reasoning test is designed to assess your ability to work swiftly and accurately through the questions. TOP TIP: It is important that you READ the questions carefully. The questions are relatively simple but they can catch you out if you do not read them properly;

- *Verbal Ability* – it is important that you brush up on your verbal reasoning skills. Working in the Royal Navy requires an ability to communicate effectively and demonstrate precision, accuracy and intelligence. TOP TIP: Other ways of improving your ability include carrying out crosswords, word searches or any other means that require an ability to work with the English language;

- *Numerical Reasoning* – you will be assessed on your ability to deal with numbers and sequences. Make sure that you carry out plenty of practice questions regarding multiplication, division, ratios, fractions, percentages, areas, number sequences, charts and graphs etc;

- *Mechanical Reasoning* – working in the Royal Navy will require strong levels of technical and mechanical understanding. Make sure that you practice these questions until you feel confident with the different types of questions that may appear in your assessment;

- Practice your speed as well as your accuracy. Remember, the tests are timed, so you want to ensure that you have answered a sufficient amount of questions in the allotted time;

- Eliminate the most obscure answers first. This will save you time. By eliminating the answers you know to be incorrect, will narrow down the choices of possible correct answers.

WHAT DO THE QUESTIONS LOOK LIKE?

Below are example questions of the Royal Navy Recruiting Test questions that you will be assessed on.

REASONING

EXAMPLE 1

Work out which option fits best in the missing square in order to complete the sequence.

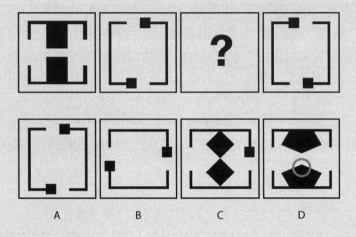

A   B   C   D

How to work it out

- In the above example, you will notice that every even box (2 and 4) shows each shape being reflected horizontally. Box 1 and box 3 need to be following the same pattern, it contains a black shape, inside open brackets;

- Therefore the answer needs to contain a black shape, inside open brackets.

Answer

D

REASONING

EXAMPLE 2

Work out which number completes the number sequence.

7 10 14 19 25 ?

How to work it out

- You need to find the pattern linking each of the numbers. Sometimes there may only be one pattern, or sometimes there may be more than one pattern;

- In the example above, the numbers increase by 3, then 4, then 5, then 6, and so forth, so the next number in the sequence needs to be increased from 25 by 7, giving you the answer of 32.

Answer

32

EXAMPLE 3

Work out which word is missing in order to complete the sentence.

Mountain is to climb as slope is to...

How to work it out

- You need to work out how the words are linked;
- For example, you **climb** a mountain, so you would **ski** on a slope.

Answer

Ski

REASONING

EXAMPLE 4

Work out which word is missing in order to complete the sentence.

Rich is the antonym of ...

How to work it out

- Antonym means opposite, so you need to find a word that means the opposite to 'rich', which would be 'poor'.

VERBAL ABILITY

EXAMPLE 1

Identify which word is the odd one out.

A – Sword
B – Dagger
C – Arrow
D – Spear
E – Shield

How to work it out

- You need to work out which word is the odd one out;
- Pay attention to how the words can be linked or relate to one another.

In the above example, you should be able to notice that 'sword', 'dagger', 'arrow' and 'spear' are all *types of weaponry,* whereas 'shield' is a *protective measurement*, and therefore is the odd one out.

Answer:

Shield

VERBAL ABILITY

EXAMPLE 2

In the sentence, the word outside the brackets will only go with three of the words inside the brackets in order to make longer words. Which **ONE** word will it **NOT** go with?

Down

A	B	C	D
(Out)	(Size)	(Ward)	(Load)

How to work it out

- You need to work out whether or not the word outside the bracket, in this case (down), can make a new word if joined with the words inside of the brackets;

- *Downsize* can be made. *Downward* can be made. *Download* can be made. *Downout* is **NOT** a word and therefore does not work.

Answer:

A = Out

VERBAL ABILITY

EXAMPLE 3

In each question, there are four or five words, your job is to pick out the word that links all of the other words together.

A	B	C	D
Trousers	Clothing	Shirt	Skirt

How to work it out

- You need to work out which word can group all of the other words to form a word family.

For the above example, 'clothing' is the word that links 'trousers', 'skirt' and 'shirt' (they are all items of clothing), so therefore the correct answer would be B.

Answer:

B = clothing

VERBAL ABILITY

EXAMPLE 4

The following sentence has one word missing. Which ONE word makes the best sense when placed in the sentence?

The man took his dog for a _ _ _ _ _ _ _ walk.

A – Boring

B – Daily

C – Funny

D – Dangerous

E – Running

How to work it out

- You need to work out which word, out of the answer options available, fits in with the structure of the sentence;

- Pay attention to past, present and future tenses;

- Pay attention to spelling!

- Pay attention to whether or not the sentence makes sense after adding in the new word.

Answer:

B = Daily

NUMERICAL REASONING

EXAMPLE 1

Add these fractions.

$$\frac{5}{7} + \frac{3}{5}$$

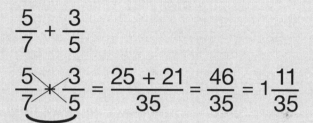

$$\frac{5}{7} \times \frac{3}{5} = \frac{25 + 21}{35} = \frac{46}{35} = 1\frac{11}{35}$$

Crossbow Method:

- The CROSS looks like a multiplication sign and it tells you which numbers to multiply together.
- One arm is saying 'multiply the 5 by the 5', and the other arm is saying 'multiply the 7 by the 3'.
- The BOW says 'multiply the 7 by the 5'.
- So the correct answer would be 1 11/35

EXAMPLE 2

Subtract these fractions.

$$\frac{4}{7} - \frac{2}{5}$$

$$\frac{4}{7} \times \frac{2}{5} = \frac{20 - 14}{35} = \frac{6}{35}$$

- To subtract fractions, the method is exactly the same. The only difference is, you minus the two numbers forming the top of the fraction, as opposed to adding them.

NUMERICAL REASONING

EXAMPLE 3

Multiply these fractions.

$$\frac{2}{3} \times \frac{4}{7}$$

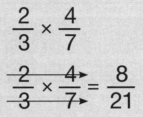

$$\frac{2}{3} \times \frac{4}{7} = \frac{8}{21}$$

Arrow Method:

- Multiplying fractions is easy. Draw an arrow through the two top numbers of the fraction, and then draw an arrow through the two bottom numbers (like shown above) and then multiply – simple!

- Sometimes the fraction can be simplified, but in the above example, the answer is already in its simplest form.

EXAMPLE 4

Divide these fractions.

$$\frac{3}{7} \div \frac{1}{3}$$

$$\frac{3}{7} \times \frac{3}{1} = \frac{3}{7} \times \frac{3}{1} = \frac{9}{7} = 1\frac{2}{7}$$

- Most people think that dividing fractions is difficult, but it's not! It's relatively simple if you have mastered multiplying fractions.

- Mathematicians realised that if you turned the second fraction upside down (as in the above example), and then change the 'divide' sum to a 'multiply', you will get the correct answer, every time!

NUMERICAL REASONING

EXAMPLE 5

<u>Rounding up to Significant Figures:</u>

What is 7.9942 to two significant figures?

- In the above example, you have to round up.

- The two significant figures are 7 and 9. The digit after the 9 is 9, so we have to round up to 8.00.

<u>Rounding up to Decimal Places:</u>

What is 2.6249 to three decimal places?

- This is simple, if the question asks you to round up to three decimal places, you count the numbers of decimal places, in this case 3, and then use the next number to either round up or round down.

- The answer would be 2.625

- The 9 after the 4 tells you that you need to round up the 4 to a 5. So 2.624 (because of the 9), will become 2.625

NUMERICAL REASONING

EXAMPLE 6

$$\frac{1}{10} = 0.1 = 10\%$$

How to convert fractions into decimals into percentages:

- To change 0.1 into a percentage, you would move the decimal point two places to the right, so it becomes 10%.

- To convert 1/10 into a decimal, you would divide both numbers. For example, $1 \div 10 = 0.1$.

- To convert 10% into a decimal, you move the decimal point two places to the left. For example, to convert 10% into a decimal, the decimal point moves two spaces to the left to become 0.1.

MECHANICAL COMPREHENSION

EXAMPLE 1

If the pulley is fixed, then the force required is equal to the weight. A simple way to work out how to calculate the force that is required, is to divide the weight by the number of sections of rope supporting it.

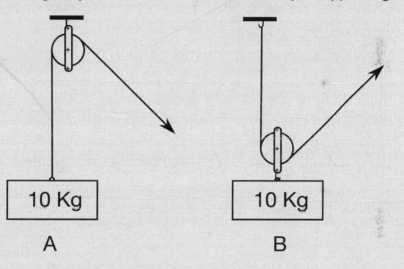

Diagram A = there is only one section of rope supporting the weight, therefore this can be worked out by = 10 ÷ 1 = 10.

Diagram B = there are two ropes supporting the weight, therefore this can be worked out by: 10 (weight) ÷ 2 (number of ropes supporting the weight) = 5.

MECHANICAL COMPREHENSION

EXAMPLE 2

When springs are arranged in a series, each spring can be the subject of the force applied. If the springs are arranged in a parallel line, the force is divided equally between them.

No Force Applied

Tension Applied

Compression Applied

No Force Applied

MECHANICAL COMPREHENSION

EXAMPLE 3

If gears are connected by a chain or belt, then the gears will all move in the same direction.

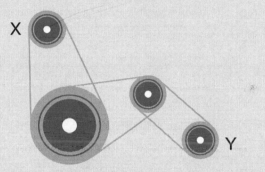

If the gears are touching (as shown in the example below), then adjacent gears move in the opposite direction. In the example, X and Y will move in opposite directions.

MECHANICAL COMPREHENSION

EXAMPLE 4

Questions regarding circuits usually follow a similar circuit, which will include: a power source, switches, bulbs and a path of wiring.

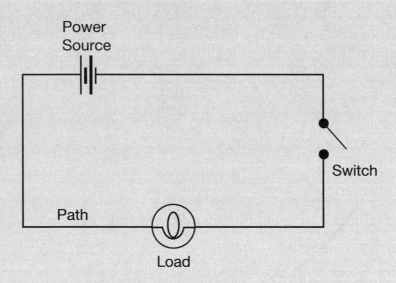

ROYAL NAVY RECRUITING TEST – REASONING

TEST SECTION 1

> *You have 10 minutes in which to complete the 20 questions. Please note that the time limit placed on this exercise will not be the same as the one set during the real Royal Navy Recruiting Test.*

Question 1

Work out which option is a reflection of the Question Figure.

Question Figure

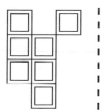

Answer Figures

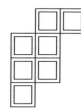 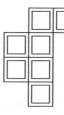 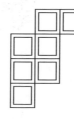 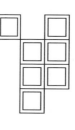

| A | B | C | D |

Answer [   ]

Question 2

Work out which option (A, B, C or D) would NOT look like the Question Figure if it was rotated.

Question Figure   Answer Figures

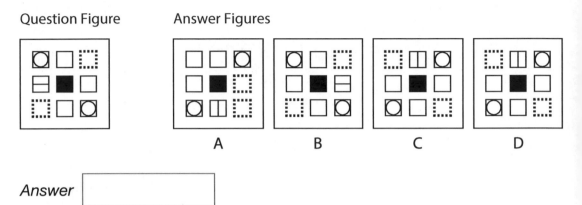

A   B   C   D

Answer

Question 3

What figure completes the sequence pattern?

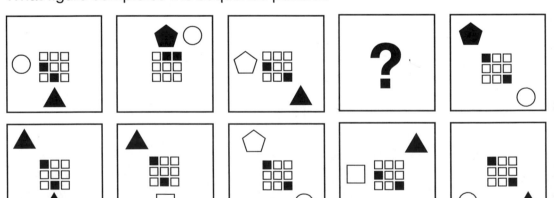

A   B   C   D   E

Answer

Question 4

What figure completes the sequence pattern?

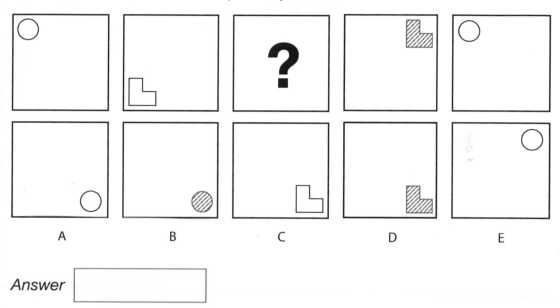

Answer [   ]

Question 5

If the following words were arranged in alphabetical order, which word would come first? <u>Please circle the correct answer.</u>

A	B	C	D	E
Astounding	Abysmal	Agitate	Aghast	Apocryphal

Question 6

Hayley sleeps for 10 hours and Julie sleeps for 650 minutes. Who sleeps the longest?

Answer [   ]

Question 7

Ben joined the Royal Navy on October the 3rd 1997 and left nine years later. Andy joined the Royal Navy on January the 25th 1993 and left on January the 25th 2003. Who stayed in the Royal Navy the longest?

Answer

Question 8

What comes next in the sequence?

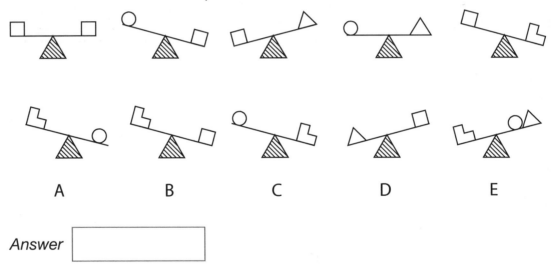

A   B   C   D   E

Answer

Question 9

Michael rides his bike twice the speed of Daniel. Who rides their bike the fastest?

Answer

Question 10

What comes next in the sequence?

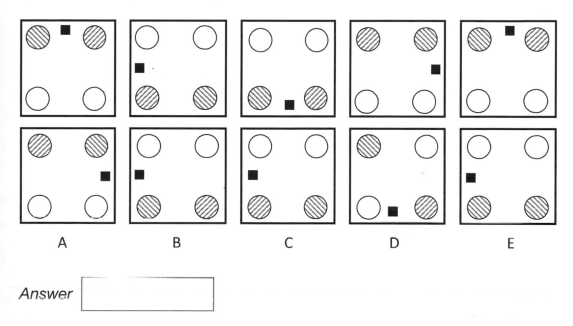

A   B   C   D   E

Answer

Question 11

Sandra has had her driving license a quarter of the time of Rachel. Who has held their driving license for the shortest time?

Answer

Question 12

Look carefully for the pattern, and then choose which pair of numbers comes next.

1   4   9   16   25   36   49

A. 54, 63

B. 63, 74

C. 51, 80

D. 56, 82

E. 64, 81

Answer [   ]

Question 13

Look carefully for the pattern, and then choose which pair of numbers comes next.

1   8   27   90   64   125   216

A. 90, 343

B. 343, 512

C. 343, 90

D. 90, 512

E. 380, 418

Answer [   ]

Question 14

Fill in the missing gap in order to complete the sequence.

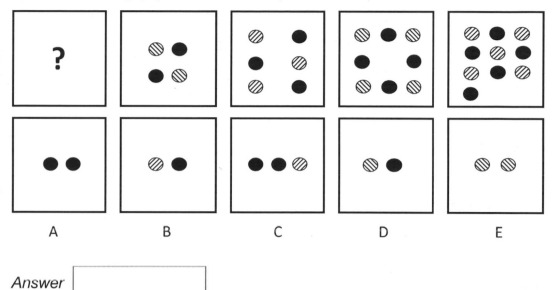

A   B   C   D   E

Answer

Question 15

What comes next in the sequence?

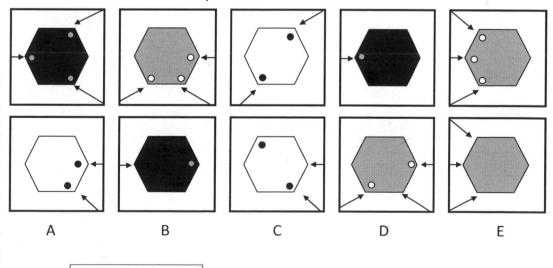

A   B   C   D   E

Answer

Question 16

Look carefully for the pattern, and then choose which pair of numbers comes next.

0 7 7 14 21 35 56

A. 91, 147

B. 90, 146

C. 65, 125

D. 65, 121

E. 65, 136

Answer

Question 17

Look carefully for the pattern, and then choose which pair of numbers comes next.

9 18 27 36 45 54 63

A. 73, 82

B. 72, 80

C. 81, 90

D. 72, 81

E. None of the above

Answer

Question 18

Which word contains the most vowels?

A	B	C	D	E
Movement	Performance	Fulfilment	Belittle	Manoeuvre

Question 19

Jamie is shyer than Rose. Who is more confident?

Answer [   ]

Question 20

If the following words were arranged in alphabetical order, which word would come last? <u>Please circle the correct answer.</u>

A	B	C	D	E
Petrified	Petroleum	Penalised	Pewter	Perpendicular

ROYAL NAVY RECRUIT TEST REASONING – TEST SECTION 1 ANSWERS

Q1. D

EXPLANATION = Figures A, B and C are all manipulations of the shape; they're not reflections. Figure D is a reflection of the Question Figure.

Q2. A

EXPLANATION = Figure A is the correct answer because it is not identical to the Question Figure. The dotted squares should be diagonal to one another, however this figure places them side by side.

Q3. B

Rule 1 = the position of the large shape is determined by the small, black squares.

Rule 2 = for the large shapes; one shape has to be white, and the other has to be black.

Figure A can be ruled out because both the large shapes are black; there should be one large shape that is white. Figure C can be ruled out because both the large shapes are white; there should be one large shape that is black. Figure D can be ruled out because the black triangle should be positioned in the bottom right corner (the small black square determines the place of the large shape). Figure E can be ruled out because the white circle should be positioned in the top left corner (the small black square determines the place of the large shape).

Q4. B

Rule 1 = the shapes move one corner anti-clockwise as the sequence progresses.

Rule 2 = the shapes alternate from a circle to an 'L' shape.

Rule 3 = the colour pattern alternates from white, white, patterned, patterned and then repeats.

Q5. B = abysmal

EXPLANATION = 'abysmal' would be the first word. If the words were arranged in alphabetical order, they would read as follows: *abysmal, aghast, agitate, apocryphal* and *astounding*.

Q6. Julie

EXPLANATION = Julie sleeps for 10 hours and 50 minutes, whereas Hayley sleeps for 10 hours. Therefore Julie sleeps for the longest amount of time.

Q7. Andy

EXPLANATION = Ben spent 9 years in the Royal Navy, whereas Andy spent 10 years in the Royal Navy. Therefore, Andy spent longer in the Royal Navy.

Q8. C

Rule 1 = squares weigh more than the circles.

Rule 2 = squares weigh more than the triangles.

Rule 3 = triangles and circles weigh the same.

Rule 3 = 'L' shapes weigh more than the squares.

Figure A can be ruled out because the 'L' shape weighs more than circles, therefore the scales are not correct. Figure B can be ruled out because the 'L' shape weighs more than squares; and therefore the scales are incorrect. Figure D can be ruled out because squares weigh more than triangles. Figure E can be ruled out because you are not given any indication as to whether the circle and the triangle would weigh more than the 'L' shape.

Q9. Michael

EXPLANATION = Michael rides his bike twice as fast as Daniel.

Q10. C

Rule 1 = the black square rotates 90° anti-clockwise.

Rule 2 = the downward hatching circle follows the pattern of: top left, bottom right, bottom left, top right. The sequence then repeats.

Rule 3 = the upward hatching circle follows the pattern of: top right, bottom left, bottom right, top left. The sequence then repeats.

Q11. Sandra

EXPLANATION = Sandra has had her license a quarter of the time of Rachel. So if Rachel has had her license for 12 years, that means Sandra would only have had her license for 3 years.

Q12. E

EXPLANATION = the regular series is based on square numbers. The sequence starts from (1 x 1), (2 x 2), (3 x 3), (4 x 4) and so on.

Q13. A

EXPLANATION = this is a cube numbered sequence, with an alternating addition series, in which a random number, 90, is interpolated as every fourth number. The regular sequence follows the pattern of (1 x 1 x 1), (2 x 2 x 2), (3 x 3 x 3), (4 x 4 x 4) and so on.

Q14. B

Rule 1 = the number of dots increase by 2 each time.

Rule 2 = the diagonal lines alternate from top left to bottom right; to top right to bottom left.

Rule 3 = the number of black dots increase by 1 each time.

Figure A can be ruled out because the first figure should contain one black dot and one striped dot. Figure C can be ruled out because the figure should contain only two dots, not three. Figure D can be ruled out because the diagonal lines are going the wrong way; they should be top right to bottom left; not top left to bottom right. Figure E can be ruled out because there should be one black dot and one striped dot.

Q15. A

Rule 1 = the hexagon alternates colour. It changes colour from black, grey, white, black, grey, white and so forth.

Rule 2 = the black arrows must be touching the outer squared box.

Rule 3 = the black arrows are used to indicate where the circles should be inside the hexagon.

Rule 4 = the circles inside the shapes follow the colour pattern of: grey, white, black, grey, white, black and so forth.

Q16. A = 91, 147

EXPLANATION = this is a Fibonacci number sequence. The sequence follows the pattern of adding the two previous numbers together. For example, the 21 is found by adding the 14 and the 7 together.

Q17. D = 72, 81

EXPLANATION = the sequence follows the pattern of multiplying the number by 9 to give you the next number in the sequence.

Q18. E = manoeuvre

EXPLANATION = 'manoeuvre' contains five vowels. No other answer option contains more vowels.

Q19. Rose

EXPLANATION = if Jamie is shyer than Rose, that means Rose is more confident.

Q20. E = pewter

EXPLANATION = 'pewter' would be the word that comes last. If the words were arranged in alphabetical order, they would read as follows: *penalised, perpendicular, petrified, petroleum* and *pewter.*

ROYAL NAVY RECRUITING TEST – REASONING

TEST SECTION 2

> *You have 10 minutes in which to complete the 20 questions. Please note that the time limit placed on this exercise will not be the same as the one set during the real Royal Navy Recruiting Test.*

Question 1

What figure completes the sequence pattern?

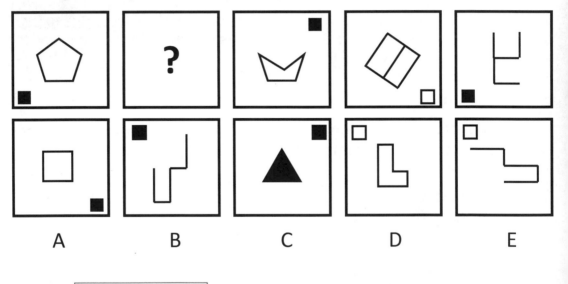

A   B   C   D   E

Answer [   ]

Question 2

What figure completes the sequence pattern?

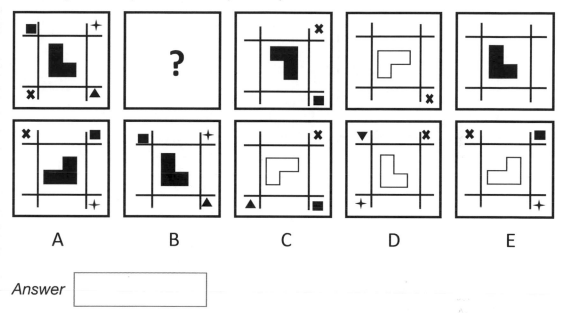

Answer [   ]

Question 3

If the following words were arranged in alphabetical order, which word would come second?

A	B	C	D	E
Imagination	Immigrate	Impose	Implement	Imitative

Question 4

Which of the following diagrams (A, B or C) comes next in the sequence?

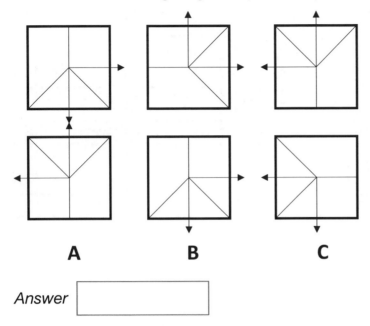

A   **B**   **C**

Answer

Question 5

Which of the following diagrams (A, B or C) comes next in the sequence?

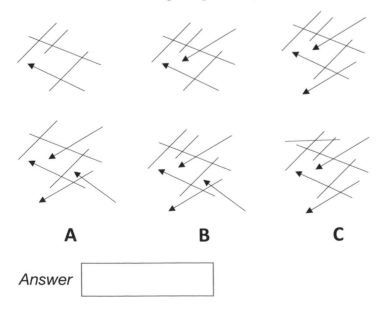

A   **B**   **C**

Answer

Question 6

Look carefully for the pattern, and then choose which number completes the sequence.

4   14   23   ?   38   44   49   53

A – 27

B – 32

C – 31

D – 35

E – 34

Answer [   ]

Question 7

Look carefully for the pattern, and then choose which number comes next.

1   42   4   38   7   32   10   24   13   ?

A – 14

B – 15

C – 16

D – 18

E – 20

Answer [   ]

Question 8

Work out which answer (A, B, C or D) is a rotation of Figure 1.

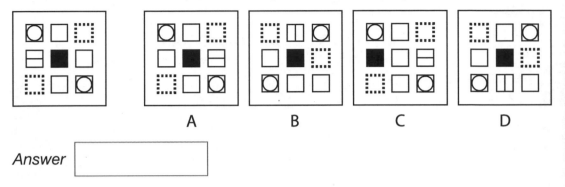

Answer [   ]

Question 9

Work out which answer (A, B, C or D) is a rotation of Figure 1.

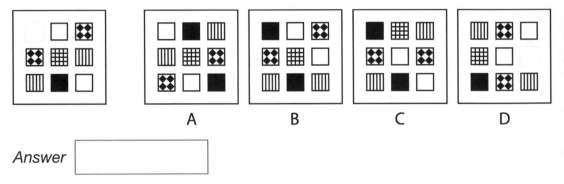

Answer [   ]

Question 10

Work out which answer (A, B, C or D) is a rotation of Figure 1.

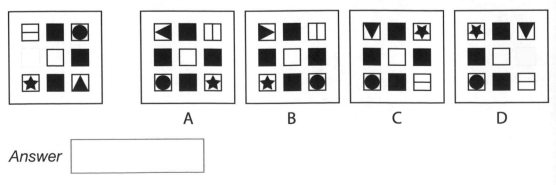

Answer [   ]

Question 11

If the following words were arranged in alphabetical order, which word would come third?

A	B	C	D	E
Address	Adopt	Addictive	Advise	Adorable

Question 12

If the following words were arranged in alphabetical order, which word would come last?

A	B	C	D	E
Befriend	Betrayal	Better	Benign	Benefit

Question 13

Phillip is stronger than Tom. Who is the weakest?

Answer

Question 14

Car is to motorway, as boat is to…

A – Water.

B – River.

C – Pond.

D – Ferry.

E – Ship.

Answer

Question 15

Sammie watches twice as much TV as Katie. Cara watches half the amount of what Katie watches. Who watches the least amount of television?

A	B	C	D
Sammie	Katie	Cara	Cannot be determined

Question 16

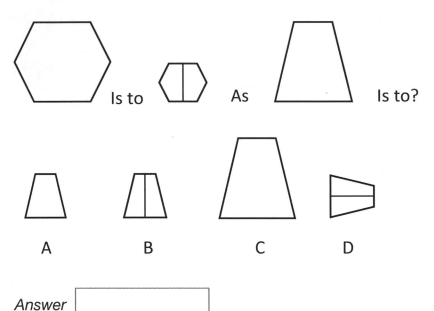

Answer [   ]

Question 17

Which of the following shapes (A, B or C) comes next in the series?

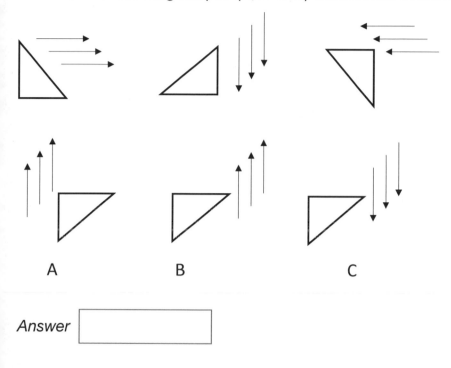

A   B   C

Answer

Question 18

Which of the following words contains the least amount of vowels?

A	B	C	D	E
Extremities	Combination	Undeniable	Fluctuate	Audacious

Question 19

Polly can run faster than George. George can run faster than David, who is slower than Michael. Michael is faster than Polly. Who is the slowest?

A	B	C	D	E
Polly	George	David	Michael	Cannot say

Question 20

Which answer fits in with the patterned sequence?

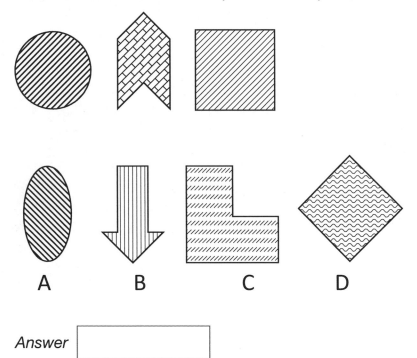

Answer [   ]

ROYAL NAVY RECRUIT TEST REASONING – TEST SECTION 2 ANSWERS

Q1. E

Rule 1 = the small square moves around one place clockwise as the sequence progresses.

Rule 2 = the small square alternates from black to white as the sequence progresses.

Rule 3 = the shape in the centre must contain 5 sides.

Figure A can be ruled out because the shape in the centre has only four sides; also, the black square in the bottom right corner should be a white square in the top left corner. Figure B can be ruled out because the black square needs to be a white square. Figure C can be ruled out because the shape in the centre needs to be five sides; also the black square in the top right corner needs to be a white square in the top left corner. Figure D can be ruled out because the shape in the centre has six sides, and it should have five sides.

Q2. E

Rule 1 = the shape in the middle rotates 90° anti-clockwise as the sequence progresses.

Rule 2 = the shape in the middle alternates from black to white as the sequence progresses.

Rule 3 = the small shapes move one corner clockwise.

Rule 4 = as the shapes rotate around, a shape is left off. You will notice, that the 'cross' shape appears the most, therefore this must be the beginning of this sequence, and so the last shape rotated (using the 'cross' to begin), will be left off.

Figure A can be ruled out because the shape in the middle needs to be white, not black. Figure B can be ruled out because the shape in the middle needs to be white, and rotated 90° anti-clockwise; also, the small shapes do not follow the correct pattern. Figure C can be ruled out because the shape in the middle needs to be rotated 180°; also, the small shapes do not follow the correct pattern. Figure D can be ruled out because the shape in the middle needs to be rotated 90° anti-clockwise; none of the small shapes are in the correct position.

Q3. E = Imitative

EXPLANATION = 'imitative' would be the second word in the sequence. If the words were arranged in alphabetical order, they would read as follows: *imagination, imitative, immigrate, implement* and *impose*.

Q4. C

EXPLANATION = as you can see in the first row of diagrams, the shapes are rotating 90° anti-clockwise. Therefore, the next shape in the sequence needs to be rotated 90°.

Q5. B

EXPLANATION = in the sequence, one arrow is added to each diagram as the sequence progresses. Therefore, the only answer option that works is answer option B.

Q6. C = 31

EXPLANATION = the sequence begins by adding 10, then 9, then 8, then 7 and so forth. Therefore the number between 23 and 38 needs to be added by 8. So, 23 + 8 = 31.

Q7. A = 14

EXPLANATION = the numbers 1, 4, 7, 10, and 13 are increasing by 3 each time. The numbers 42, 38, 32, and 24 are being subtracted by 4, then 6, then 8 and so forth.

You need to follow the even patterned sequence, so the next number after 24 would be 24 – 10 = 14. (You would minus 10 because the sequence requires you to minus 4, then 6, then 8 and so forth).

Q8. A

EXPLANATION = Figure 1 would need to be rotated 180° to match answer option A. No other answer option is a rotation of Figure 1.

Q9. A

EXPLANATION = Figure 1 would need to be rotated 180° to match answer option A. No other answer option is a rotation of Figure 1.

Q10. C

EXPLANATION = Figure 1 would need to be rotated 180° to match answer option C. No other answer option is a rotation of Figure 1.

Q11. B = adopt

EXPLANATION = the third word would be 'adopt'. If you were to put the words in alphabetical order, they would read as follows: *addictive, address, adopt, adorable* and *advise*.

Q12. C = better

EXPLANATION = the last word would be 'better'. If you were to put the words in alphabetical order, they would read as follows: *befriend, benefit, benign, betrayal* and *better.*

Q13. Tom

EXPLANATION = if Phillip is stronger than Tom, that means Tom is the weakest of the two.

Q14. B = river

EXPLANATION = you drive a car on the motorway, as you would steer a boat on a river.

Q15. C = Cara

EXPLANATION = Sammie watches twice as much as Katie, which means Sammie watches the most. Cara watches half the amount of Katie, which means she watches 50% less than Katie, therefore Cara watches the least amount of TV.

Q16. B

EXPLANATION = the large trapezoid needs to change to a small trapezoid with a vertical line positioned down the middle of the shape.

Q17. B

EXPLANATION = answer option B is correct. The triangle is rotating 90° anti-clockwise as the sequence progresses. The arrows rotate 90° clockwise as the sequence progresses. The arrows remain on the right side of the triangle.

Q18. D = fluctuate

EXPLANATION = 'fluctuate' contains the least number of vowels; it only contains 4. Whereas all of the other words contain more vowels.

Q19. C = David

EXPLANATION = Michael is the fastest, then Polly, then George and then David. Therefore David is the slowest.

Q20. C

EXPLANATION = the pattern inside the shapes contain diagonal stripes (from bottom left to top right).

Now move on to the Verbal section of the Royal Navy Recruiting Test.

ROYAL NAVY RECRUITING TEST – VERBAL ABILITY

TEST SECTION 1

You have 8 minutes in which to complete the 20 questions. Please note that the time limit placed on this exercise will not be the same as the one set during the real Royal Navy Recruiting Test.

Question 1

Which of the following is the odd one out?

A	B	C	D	E
Sight	Height	Eight	Night	Flight

Question 2

Which of the following is the odd one out?

A	B	C	D	E
Lonely	Solitary	Secluded	Sheltered	Affable

Question 3

In the line below, the word outside of the brackets will only go with three of the words inside the brackets to make longer words. Which **one** word will it **not** go with?

Un

A	B	C	D
(interested	able	anticipated	different)

Answer [   ]

Question 4

In the line below, the word outside of the brackets will only go with three of the words inside the brackets to make longer words. Which **one** word will it **not** go with?

In

A	B	C	D
(genious	auspicious	mediate	curable)

Answer

Question 5

Which five letter word can be placed in front of the following words, in order to make four new words?

Rated   Go   Achieve   Ground

Answer

Question 6

Which four letter word can be placed in front of the following words, in order to make four new words?

Where   Thing   One   Time

Answer

Question 7

The following sentence has one word missing. Which of the following words makes the best sense of the sentence?

I can't _____ what their family must be going through.

A – Think.
B – Imagine.
C – Anything.
D – Help.
E – Like.

Answer

Question 8

Which of the following words is the odd one out?

A	B	C	D	E
First	Second	Third	Forth	Fifth

Question 9

The following sentence has one word missing. Which word makes the best sense when placed in the sentence?

She wanted a new dress for her birthday but _____ she received some pyjamas.

A – Hoped.
B – Again.
C – Replace.
D – Instead.
E – Now.

Answer

Question 10

The following sentence has one word missing. Which word makes the best sense when placed in the sentence?

The class was asked to write a poem that _____ .

A – Rimed.

B – Ryhmed.

C – Rhymed.

D – Rymed.

Answer

Question 11

Which of the following words is the odd one out?

A	B	C	D	E
Blue	Green	Violet	Beige	Orange

Question 12

In the line below, the word outside of the brackets will only go with three of the words inside the brackets to make longer words. Which **one** word will it **not** go with?

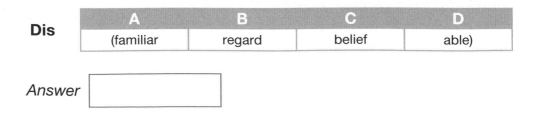

	A	B	C	D
Dis	(familiar	regard	belief	able)

Answer

Question 13

Which of the following words is the odd one out?

A	B	C	D	E
Ducks	Trees	Water	People	Books

Question 14

The following sentence has two words missing. Which two words make the best sense when placed in the sentence?

It was _____ responsibility and they had to _____ the consequences.

A – There / face.

B – Their / see.

C – Their / choose.

D – Their / face.

E – They're / find.

Answer [   ]

Question 15

Which of the following words is the odd one out?

A	B	C	D	E
Television	Microwave	Camera	Hairdryer	Cooker

Question 16

Which two letter word can be placed in front of the following words, in order to create four new words?

Personate   Plausible   Age   Port

Answer

Question 17

Which three letter word can be placed in front of the following words, in order to create four new words?

End   One   Repid   Rust

Answer

Question 18

Which of the following words is the odd one out?

A	B	C	D	E
Frown	Down	Gown	Shown	Town

Question 19

The following sentence has two words missing. Which words make the best sense when placed in the sentence?

Sometimes you have to make choices _____ _____ they may not always be the correct ones.

A	B	C	D	E
Even though	Although they	Even although	Despite being	If even

Question 20

Which of the following words is the odd one out?

A	B	C	D	E
Oak	Fir	Wood	Ash	Beech

ROYAL NAVY RECRUIT TEST VERBAL ABILITY – TEST SECTION 1 ANSWERS

Q1. C = eight

EXPLANATION = 'eight' is the odd one out. Although all the words end in 'ight', 'eight' has a different sound to the rest of the words.

Q2. E = affable

EXPLANATION = 'affable' is the odd one out because all of the other words are synonyms of being lonely, whereas 'affable' refers to being sociable and friendly.

Q3. D = different

EXPLANATION = if you were to put 'un' with the words 'interested', 'able', and 'anticipated', you would get: *uninterested, unable* and *unanticipated*. However, if you were to put 'un' with 'different', this would not be grammatically correct; this would need to be 'indifferent'.

Q4. C = mediate

EXPLANATION = if you were to put 'in' with the words 'genious', 'auspicious' and 'curable', you would get: *ingenious, inauspicious* and *incurable*. However, if you tried to put 'in' with 'mediate', this would be grammatically incorrect.

Q5. Under

EXPLANATION = *under*rated, *under*go, *under*achieve and *under*ground.

Q6. Some

EXPLANATION = *some*where, *some*thing, *some*one and *some*time.

Q7. B = imagine

EXPLANATION = the word that would best complete the sentence would be 'imagine'. So the sentence would read: *'I can't **imagine** what their family must be going through'.*

Q8. D = forth

EXPLANATION = 'forth' is the odd one out because it is spelt incorrectly. In the sequence, it refers to numbers, so therefore it should be 'fourth' not 'forth'. 'Forth' is a word used to describe moving onwards in time.

Q9. D = instead

EXPLANATION = the correct word that can be used in order to complete the sentence is 'instead'. The sentence would read as follows: *'She wanted a new dress for her birthday but **instead** she received some pyjamas'.*

Q10. C = rhymed

EXPLANATION = the word that would best complete the sentence would be 'rhymed', *'The class was asked to write a poem that **rhymed'.***

Q11. D = beige

EXPLANATION = 'beige' is the odd one out because it is not a colour of the rainbow.

Q12. A = familiar

EXPLANATION = if you were to put 'dis' with the words 'regard', 'belief', and 'able', you would get: *disregard, disbelief* and *disable*. However, if you were to put 'dis' with 'familiar', this would not be grammatically correct; it would need to be 'unfamiliar'.

Q13. C = water

EXPLANATION = 'water' is the odd one out because water cannot be counted; all of the other words can be counted i.e. number of ducks, number of trees etc.

Q14. D = their / face

EXPLANATION = the sentence would best read as follows: *'It was **their** responsibility and they had to **face** the consequences.'*

Q15. C = camera

EXPLANATION = 'camera' is the odd one out because all of the other words refer to a household appliance, whereas a camera is not a household appliance.

Q16. Im

EXPLANATION = *im*personate, *im*plausible, *im*age and *im*port.

Q17. Int

EXPLANATION = *int*end, *int*one, *int*repid and *int*rust.

Q18. D = shown

EXPLANATION = 'shown' is the odd one out because all of the other words rhyme, whereas 'shown' does not have the same tone as the other words, despite them all ending in 'own'.

Q19. A = even though

EXPLANATION = the sentence would best read as follows: *'Sometimes you have to make choices **even though** they may not always be the correct ones'.*

Q20. C = wood

EXPLANATION = 'wood' is the odd one out because all of the other words refer to *types* of wood, whereas 'wood' is the word that combines these words together.

ROYAL NAVY RECRUITING TEST – VERBAL ABILITY

TEST SECTION 2

> *You have 8 minutes in which to complete the 20 questions. Please note that the time limit placed on this exercise will not be the same as the one set during the real Royal Navy Recruiting Test.*

Question 1

Which five letter word can be placed in front of the following words, in order to create four new words?

Rents   Mines   Mined   Gency

Answer [   ]

Question 2

The following sentence has two words missing. Which words make the best sense when placed in the sentence?

The train service has _____ customers that there may be several delays because of _____ difficulties.

A – Informed / financial.

B – Said / rail.

C – Stated / track.

D – Requested / electrical.

E – Informed / technical.

Answer [   ]

Question 3

In the line below, the word outside of the brackets will only go with three of the words inside the brackets to make longer words. Which one word will it not go with?

	A	B	C	D
Pla	(giarise	ster	able	cebos)

Answer

Question 4

Which of the following words is the odd one out?

A	B	C	D	E
Treasure	Grass	Ship	Skull	Map

Question 5

Which four letter word can be placed at the end of the following words, in order to create four new words?

King   Parent   Adult   Liveli

Answer

Question 6

Which four letter word can be placed at the end of the following words, in order to create four new words?

Accept   Charit   Foresee   Float

Answer

Question 7

The following sentence has one word missing. Which one word makes the best sense when placed in the sentence?

He needed to be _____ for what he had done.

A – Helped.

B – Reprimanded.

C – Stopped.

D – Sentenced.

E – Custody.

Answer

Question 8

In the line below, the word outside of the brackets will only go with three of the words inside the brackets to make longer words. Which one word will it not go with?

	A	B	C	D
Per	(cipient	meable	fecting	atical)

Answer

Question 9

Which of the following words is the odd one out?

A	B	C	D	E
Grass	Flowers	Worms	Mud	Beetle

Question 10

The following sentence has one word missing. Which one word makes the best sense of the sentence?

Sarah was the manager of a company and .... all types of problems.

A – Encountered.

B – Incountered.

C – in counter.

D – Encownter.

E – Encountre.

Answer [   ]

Question 11

Which of the following words is the odd one out?

A	B	C	D	E
Pence	Pounds	Euros	Coins	Dime

Question 12

In the line below, the word outside of the brackets will only go with three of the words inside the brackets to make longer words. Which one word will it not go with?

	A	B	C	D
Bru	(ken	shed	talities	nette)

Answer [   ]

Question 13

Which two letter word can be placed in front of the following words, in order to create four new words?

Polar *Sexual* *Nary* *Cep*

Answer [   ]

Question 14

Which five letter word can be placed in front of the following words, in order to create four new words?

Vening *Vision* *Size* *Sede*

Answer [   ]

Question 15

Which of the following words is the odd one out?

A	B	C	D	E
Prestigious	Reputable	Important	Admired	Insignificant

Question 16

Which of the following words is the odd one out?

A	B	C	D	E
Cup	Fork	Knife	Teaspoon	Spoon

Question 17

The following sentence has two words missing. Which words make the best sense when placed in the sentence?

We are about to _____ upon a _____ adventure.

A – Go / treacherous.

B – Join / treacherous.

C – Board / different.

D – Embark / treacherous.

E – Head / wild.

Answer [   ]

Question 18

The following sentence has one word missing. Which word makes the best sense when placed in the sentence?

I find it difficult to _____ Mia's reasons for marrying him.

A – Clarify.

B – Comprehend.

C – Utilise.

D – State.

E – Illustrate.

Answer [   ]

Question 19

In the line below, the word outside of the brackets will only go with three of the words inside the brackets to make longer words. Which one word will it not go with?

Pro

A	B	C	D
(voke	active	test	date)

Answer

Question 20

The following sentence has one word missing. Which word makes the best sense of the sentence?

It was an _____ first kiss.

A – Good.

B – Pleasing.

C – Uninteresting.

D – Unforgettable.

E – Undeniable.

Answer

ROYAL NAVY RECRUIT TEST VERBAL ABILITY – TEST SECTION 2 ANSWERS

Q1. Deter

EXPLANATION = *deter*rents, *deter*mines, *deter*mined and *deter*gency.

Q2. E = informed / technical

EXPLANATION = the sentence would best read as follows: '*The train service has **informed** customers that there may be several delays because of **technical** difficulties'.*

Q3. C = able

EXPLANATION = if you were to put 'pla' with the words 'giarise', 'ster' and 'cebos', you would get: *plagiarise, plaster,* and *placebos*. However, if you tried to put 'pla' with 'able', this would be grammatically incorrect.

Q4. B = grass

EXPLANATION = 'grass' is the odd one out because all of the other words refer to pirates, whereas 'grass' has no clear relationship with any of the words.

Q5. Hood

EXPLANATION = king*hood*, parent*hood*, adult*hood* and liveli*hood*.

Q6. Able

EXPLANATION = accept*able*, charit*able*, foresee*able* and float*able*.

Q7. B = reprimanded

EXPLANATION = the sentence would read best as follows: '*He needed to be **reprimanded** for what he had done'.*

Q8. D = atical

EXPLANATION = if you were to put 'per' with the words 'cipient', 'meable' and 'fecting', you would get: *percipient, permeable* and *perfecting.* However, if you tried to put 'per' with 'atical', this would be grammatically incorrect; it would need to be 'piratical' instead.

Q9. D = mud

EXPLANATION = 'mud' is the odd one out because all of the other words refer to living organisms.

Q10. A = encountered

EXPLANATION = the sentence would best read as follows: *'Sarah was the manager of a company and **encountered** all types of problems'.*

Q11. D = coins

EXPLANATION = 'coins' is the odd one out because this word groups all of the other words; the rest of the words are all *types* of coins.

Q12. A = ken

EXPLANATION = if you were to put 'bru' with the words 'shed', 'talities' and 'nette', you would get: *brushed, brutalities* and *brunette.* However, if you tried to put 'bru' with 'ken', this would be grammatically incorrect; this would need to be 'broken' instead.

Q13. Bi

EXPLANATION = *bi*polar, *bi*sexual, *bi*nary and *bi*cep.

Q14. Super

EXPLANATION = *super*vening, *super*vision, *super*size and *super*sede.

Q15. E = insignificant

EXPLANATION = 'insignificant' is the odd one out because all of the other words are used to describe something of 'prestige value'. Whereas 'insignificant' is the opposite.

Q16. A = cup

EXPLANATION = 'cup' is the odd one out because all of the other words are types of cutlery, whereas a 'cup' is an item of crockery.

Q17. D = embark / treacherous

EXPLANATION = the sentence would read best as follows: *'We are about to embark upon a treacherous adventure'.*

Q18. B = comprehend

EXPLANATION = the sentence would read best as follows: *'I find it difficult to comprehend Mia's reasons for marrying him'.*

Q19. D = date

EXPLANATION = if you were to put 'pro' with the words 'voke', 'active' and 'test', you would get: *provoke, proactive* and *protest*. However, if you tried to put 'pro' with 'date', this would be grammatically incorrect.

Q20. D = unforgettable

EXPLANATION = the sentence would best read as follows: *'It was an unforgettable first kiss'.*

Now move on to the Mechanical Comprehension section of the Royal Navy Recruiting Test.

ROYAL NAVY RECRUITING TEST – MECHANICAL COMPREHENSION

TEST SECTION 1

You have 12 minutes in which to complete the 20 questions. Please note that the time limit placed on this exercise will not be the same as the one set during the real Royal Navy Recruiting Test.

Question 1

What would happen to the other bulbs in the circuit if bulb X is broken?

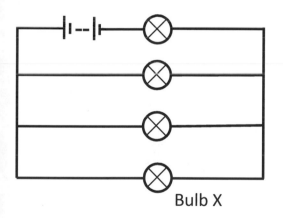

Bulb X

A	B	C	D
Stay lit, but dims	Stay lit, with same brightness	Stay lit, and brightens	No bulbs will illuminate

Question 2

In the following electrical circuit, if switch B closes, what will happen?

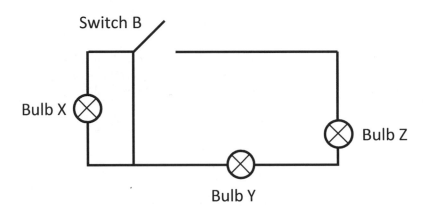

A – Bulbs X, Y, and Z will illuminate.

B – Bulb X will illuminate only.

C – Bulbs Y and Z will illuminate.

D – No bulbs will illuminate.

Answer

Question 3

In the following circuit, if bulb 3 is removed and the switch is closed, which bulbs will illuminate?

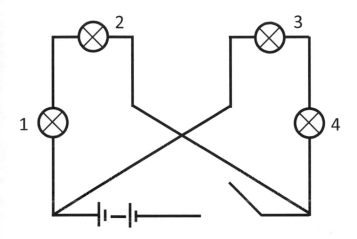

A – Bulb 4 will illuminate.

B – Bulbs 1, 2 and 4 will illuminate.

C – Bulbs 2 and 4 will illuminate.

D – Bulbs 1 and 2 will illuminate.

E – No bulbs will illuminate.

Answer

Question 4

In the following diagram, three light bulbs are connected to the same battery. Which of the following could you do to the circuit to increase the current being measured at point X?

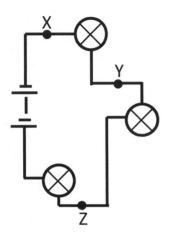

A – Increase the resistance of one of the bulbs.

B – Increase the resistance of two bulbs.

C – Add another bulb.

D – Remove one of the bulbs.

E – Increase the resistance of all three bulbs.

Answer

Question 5

Which man is carrying the most weight?

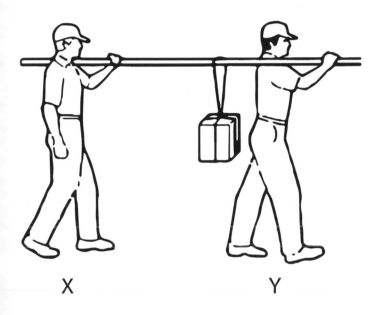

X   Y

A – X.

B – Y.

C – Both the same.

Answer

Question 6

What is the mechanical advantage in the following diagram?

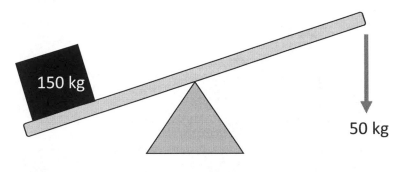

A	B	C	D	E
2	50	3	7,500	150

Question 7

How much force is required to lift the load?

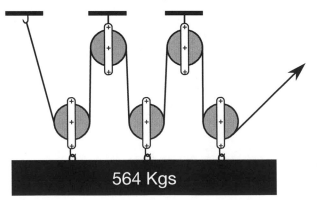

A – 282 kg.

B – 564 kg.

C – 94 kg.

D – 6 kg.

E – 76 kg.

Answer

Question 8

In the diagram, the spring can be stretched 1 inch by a force of 500 pounds. How much force needs to be applied to the object in order to move the object 4.5 inches to the left?

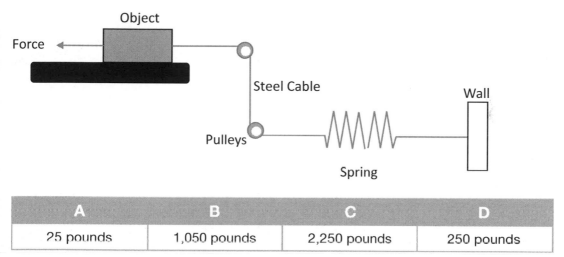

A	B	C	D
25 pounds	1,050 pounds	2,250 pounds	250 pounds

Question 9

Which nail is likely to pull out last?

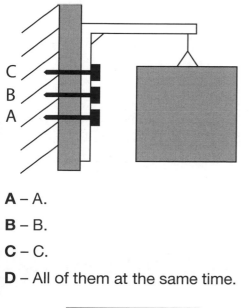

A – A.

B – B.

C – C.

D – All of them at the same time.

Answer

Question 10

In this belt and cog configuration, which cog will rotate the most number of times in twenty minutes?

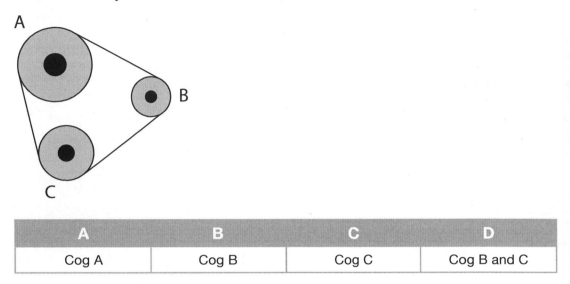

A	B	C	D
Cog A	Cog B	Cog C	Cog B and C

Question 11

How far would you have to pull the rope up to lift the weight 14 feet?

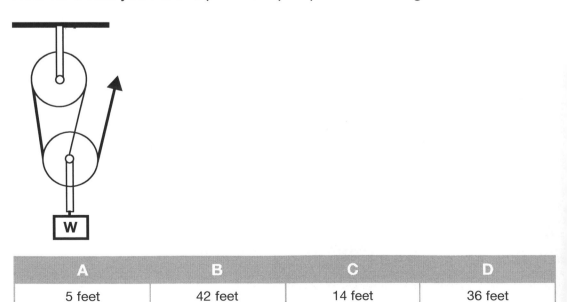

A	B	C	D
5 feet	42 feet	14 feet	36 feet

Question 12

A possible cause of an open circuit would be?

A – A loose component mount.

B – A pin pushed out of a connector.

C – A corroded connection.

D – All of the above.

Answer

[   ]

Question 13

What is the voltage if a current of 3.5 A flows through a 28 W lightbulb?

A	B	C	D	E
8 volts	98 volts	4 volts	24 volts	0.15 volts

Question 14

In the following circuit, if switches A and B are closed, and bulb B is removed, which bulbs will illuminate?

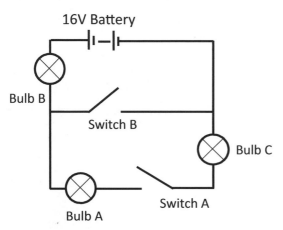

A – Bulb A only.

B – Bulb C only.

C – Bulbs A and C only.

D – No bulbs will illuminate.

Answer

Question 15

In the following circuit, how many switches need to close to light up 3 bulbs?

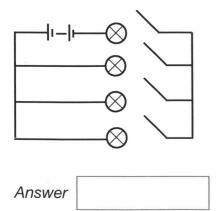

Answer

Question 16

If rope A is pulled in the direction of the arrow, which way will wheel C turn?

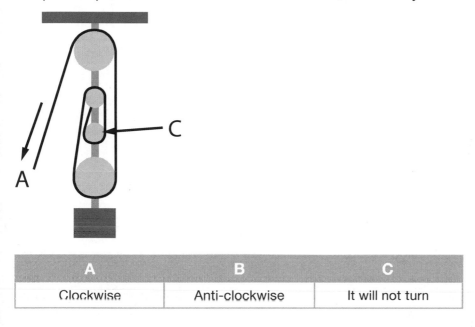

A	B	C
Clockwise	Anti-clockwise	It will not turn

Question 17

A thick block of wood rests on an even and level surface. What is the mechanical principle that makes it more difficult to push a block sideways across a surface of carpet?

A – Spring force.

B – Frictional force.

C – Gravitational force.

D – Air resistance force.

E – cannot say.

Answer [   ]

Question 18

A screw has 8 threads per inch. How many full turns are required for the nut to travel 5 inches?

A – 8 turns.

B – 5 turns.

C – 40 turns.

D – 20 turns.

E – 10 turns.

Answer

Question 19

Two triangles are placed under water and are fixed in position. Which triangle has a greater force to be exerted?

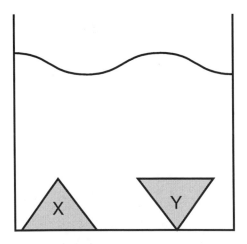

A	B	C	D
X	Y	Cannot say	Both the same

Question 20

The glass container at the very top contains water and oil. If you were to add more water, what would the container look like?

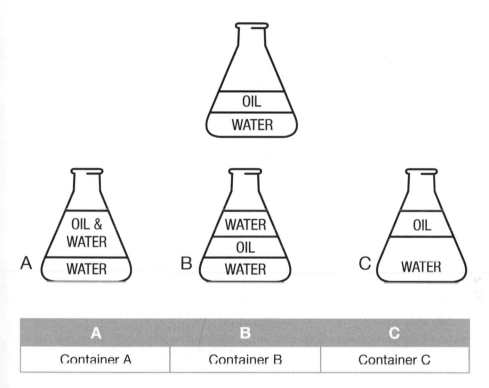

A	B	C
Container A	Container B	Container C

ROYAL NAVY RECRUIT TEST MECHANICAL COMPREHENSION – TEST SECTION 1 ANSWERS

Q1. B = stay lit, with the same brightness

EXPLANATION = if bulb X goes out, it will not affect the other bulbs. The bulbs are all placed on different paths which are linked by the same battery. Therefore, if one path stops working, the others will continue to work. This does not affect the brightness of the bulbs as the bulbs are still powered by the same amount of power coming from the battery.

Q2. D = no bulbs will illuminate

EXPLANATION = the reason that no bulbs will illuminate is because there is no power source, and therefore the bulbs would not be able to light.

Q3. D = bulbs 1 and 2 will illuminate

EXPLANATION = Bulb 4 will not illuminate because the removal of bulb 3 breaks the path of wiring, and therefore prevents bulb 4 from lighting up. The removal of bulb 3 is on a different path to bulbs and 1 and 2, and therefore does not stop them from illuminating.

Q4. D = remove one of the bulbs

EXPLANATION = if you removed one of the bulbs, this would increase the current in the circuit. The current would increase because removing a bulb from the circuit will decrease the resistance of the overall circuit.

Q5. B = Y

EXPLANATION = the majority of the weight is towards the front of the pole, therefore person Y is carrying the most weight, and person X is carrying the least amount of weight.

Q6. C = 3

EXPLANATION = in order to work out the mechanical advantage, you need to use the following method:

150 kg ÷ 50 kg = 3.

Q7. C = 94 kg

EXPLANATION = the weight has 6 supporting ropes, therefore 564 ÷ 6 = 94 kg.

Q8. C = 2,250 pounds

EXPLANATION = 4.5 multiplied by 500 = 2,250 pounds.

Q9. A = A

EXPLANATION = nail A will pull out easier because it is furthest away from the weight.

Q10. B = Cog B

EXPLANATION = cog B will rotate the most number of times in twenty minutes because it is the smallest cog, and therefore will be quicker to rotate all the way round.

Q11. B = 42 feet

EXPLANATION = 14 x 3 = 42

Q12. D = all of the above

EXPLANATION = all of the answers listed could be possible causes for an open circuit.

Q13. A = 8 volts

EXPLANATION = in order to work out the voltage, you need to use the following equation: voltage = power ÷ current = 28 ÷ 3.5 = 8.

Q14. D = no bulbs will illuminate

EXPLANATION = if bulb B is removed, it will affect the path of the circuit.

Q15. Three

EXPLANATION = three switches will need to close in order to light up three lightbulbs.

Q16. B = Anti-clockwise

EXPLANATION = if you pulled rope A downwards, Cog C would turn anti-clockwise because the rope underneath it, will be moving anti-clockwise also.

Q17. B = frictional force

EXPLANATION = friction occurs when an object is moved across a surface, resulting in resistance between the two surfaces.

Q18. C = 40 turns

EXPLANATION = 8 x 5 = 40 turns.

Q19. A = X

EXPLANATION = the pressure exerted at the base of the tank is greater than the pressure at midpoint. Therefore the pressure on the base of triangle X is greater than that of triangle Y.

Q20. C = container C

EXPLANATION = if you were to add more water, the water would sink to the bottom underneath the oil; the oil would remain on top.

Now move on to the Numerical Reasoning section of the Royal Navy Recruiting Test.

ROYAL NAVY RECRUITING TEST – NUMERICAL REASONING

TEST SECTION 1

> *You have 12 minutes in which to complete 20 questions. Please note that the time limit placed on this exercise will not be the same as the one set during the real Royal Navy Recruiting Test.*

Question 1

Simplify $x + 8x - 3x$.

A	B	C	D
$5x$	$6x$	$7x$	$12x$

Question 2

A cinema has 27 rows of seats, 28 seats in each row. Tickets are £8 each.

The cinema has sold tickets for every seat apart from 5. Estimate how much, to the nearest thousand, the cinema will make, based on the information provided?

Answer

Question 3

Work out $3/8 + 3/5$

Answer

Question 4

Work out 4/6 x 3/5

Answer

Question 5

Below is a diagram of a cube. Work out its volume in cubic centimetres.

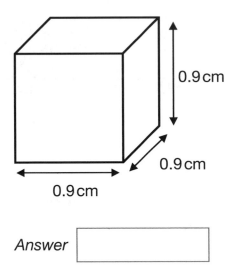

0.9 cm

0.9 cm

0.9 cm

Answer

Question 6

Three whole numbers have a total of 100. The first number is a multiple of 15. The second number is ten times the third number. Work out the three numbers.

Answer

Question 7

The probability of picking a lottery winning ticket in the national lottery is 1 in 14 million. If 36 million tickets are sold weekly, how many jackpot winners, on average, would you expect in one week?

A	B	C	D
2 million	2	20	1

Question 8

A car travelled 100 metres in 9.63 seconds. On a second occasion, it travelled 200 metres in 19.32 seconds. Which distance had the greater average speed?

A	B	C	D
100 metres	200 metres	Both the same	Cannot say

Question 9

Two of the numbers move from Box A to Box B. The total of the numbers in Box B is now four times the total of the numbers in Box A. Which two numbers move?

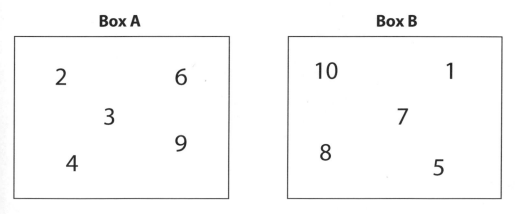

Box A	Box B
2 6	10 1
3	7
9	
4	8
	5

Answer [   ]

Question 10

Work out 256% of 6800.

Answer

Question 11

Subtract 3/8 of 104 from 5/7 of 98.

A	B	C	D
27	22	31	41

Question 12

Below is a pie chart illustrating the number of pupils studying a course in the following subject areas.

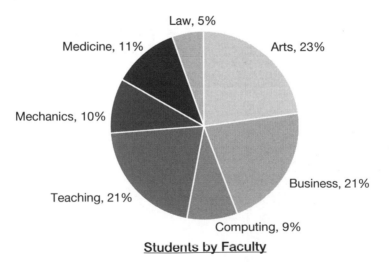

Students by Faculty

If the data is based on 3620 students, how many of those students are studying mechanics or law?

Answer

Question 13

What is 24.99653 to three significant figures?

Answer [   ]

Question 14

What is 33.968024 to three significant figures?

Answer [   ]

Question 15

What is the percentage profit or loss if the buying price is £320 and the selling price is £275.00? To the nearest whole number.

A	B	C	D
14% profit	17% profit	14% loss	12% loss

Question 16

Work out 3/5 ÷ 3/4

Answer [   ]

Question 17

Work out the following sum.

    1 3/5 + 2 3/7

A – 4 3/30

B – 6 1/6

C – 5

D – 4 1/35

Answer

Question 18

The number of times a die was cast and the number of times each individual number appeared

Casts	1	2	3	4	5	6
First 10	2	3	1	1	2	1
First 20	5	4	3	4	3	1
First 30	8	5	6	5	4	2
First 40	10	6	7	6	5	6
First 50	13	7	10	7	6	7

In no two consecutive casts did the same number appear. If the number 4 turned up in the 20th cast, which number/s could not have turned up in the 11th cast?

A	B	C	D	E
4	1	2 and 3	6	3

Question 19

Using the above table, which of the following numbers must have appeared the least amount of times in the first 50 casts?

A	B	C	D	E
2, 4 and 6	6	5	3	1

Question 20

Using the above table, if the same number occurred for the 43rd cast and the 47th cast, what number/s could it be?

A	B	C	D	E
1	2	4	1 and 6	6

ROYAL NAVY RECRUIT TEST NUMERICAL REASONING – TEST SECTION 1 ANSWERS

Q1. B = 6x

EXPLANATION = $x + 8x = 9x$. So, $9x - 3x = 6x$.

Q2. £6000

EXPLANATION = 27 rows of 28 seats = 756 – 5 (that are empty) = 751. 751 (number of seats) x £8 = £6008. To the nearest thousand = £6000.

Q3. 39/40

EXPLANATION = $\dfrac{3}{8} \ast \dfrac{3}{5} = \dfrac{15 + 24}{40} = \dfrac{39}{40}$

Q4. 12/30, 6/15 or 2/5

EXPLANATION = $\dfrac{4}{6} \times \dfrac{3}{5} = \dfrac{4 \times 3}{6 \times 5} = \dfrac{12}{30}$ or $\dfrac{6}{15}$ or $\dfrac{2}{5}$

Q5. 0.729

EXPLANATION = 0.9 x 0.9 x 0.9 = 0.729

Q6. 45, 50 and 5

EXPLANATION = three numbers with these criteria: a multiple of 15, two numbers in the ratio 10 : 1, and sum of 100.

Multiples of 15 = 15, 30, **45**, 60, 75, 90. So, the first number will be one of these numbers. Two of the numbers follow the rule of: being in the ratio 10 : 1. This works out to be 50 and 5, and will add up to 100 if you add the 45.

Q7. B = 2

EXPLANATION = 36 (million) ÷ 14 (million) = 2.57. So you could expect 2 lottery winners, on average, in a week.

Q8. A = 100 metres

EXPLANATION = 100 ÷ 9.63 = 10.384.   200 ÷ 19.32 = 10.351. Therefore 100 metres has the greatest average speed.

Q9. 9 and 4

EXPLANATION = if you moved 9 and 4, this leaves box A with a total of 11. If you add 9 and 4 to 10, 1 7, 8 and 5, you will get 44. Box B is now four times the amount of Box A.

Q10. 17408

EXPLANATION = 6800 ÷ 100 x 256 = 17408.

Q11. C = 31

EXPLANATION = 104 ÷ 8 x 3 = 39. 98 ÷ 7 x 5 = 70. So, 70 – 39 = 31.

Q12. 543

EXPLANATION = 3620 ÷ 100 x 5 = 181 (law students). 3620 ÷ 100 x 10 = 362 (mechanical students). So, the number of law and mechanical students is: 362 + 181 = 543.

Q13. 25.0

EXPLANATION = in order to work out what 24.99653 is to three significant figures, focus on the first three digits and then decide whether to round up or round down. 24.9 needs to be rounded up. This will become 25.0.

Q14. 34.0

EXPLANATION = in order to work out what 33.968024 is to three significant figures, focus on the first three digits and then decide whether to round up or round down. 33.9 needs to be rounded up. This will become 34.0.

Q15. C = 14% loss

EXPLANATION = 320 − 275 = 45.   45 ÷ 320 x 100 = 14% loss.

Q16. 12/15 or 4/5

$$\text{EXPLANATION} = \frac{3}{5} \div \frac{3}{4} = \frac{3}{5} \times \frac{4}{3} = \frac{12}{15} = \frac{4}{5}$$

Q17. D = 4 1/35

$$\text{EXPLANATION} = \frac{8}{5} \times \frac{17}{7} = \frac{56 + 85}{35} = \frac{141}{35} = 4\frac{1}{35}$$

Q18. D = 6

EXPLANATION = the question may seem tricky at first, but you should notice that the number '6' was cast once in the first 10 attempts, and only once in the first 20 attempts. Therefore, the number 6 could not have turned up in casts 11 – 20.

Q19. C = 5

EXPLANATION = the number 5 only appears 6 times in the first 50 casts, no other number has a lower cast rate at the end of 50 casts. Therefore, 5 is the number with the least amount of casts in 50 attempts.

Q20. D = 1 and 6

EXPLANATION = the numbers have to occur more than once between 30 and 40. Only the numbers 1 and 6 do this.

ROYAL NAVY RECRUITING TEST – NUMERICAL REASONING

TEST SECTION 2

> *You have 12 minutes in which to complete the 20 questions. Please note that the time limit placed on this exercise will not be the same as the one set during the real Royal Navy Recruiting Test.*

Question 1

The diagram below shows the plan of a building site. All angles are right angles.

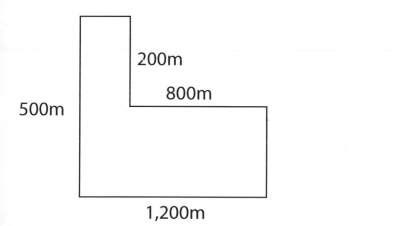

What is the area of the building site? Give your answer in hectares. 1 hectare = 10,000m² = 2.47 acres.

A	B	C	D
60 hectares	40 hectares	44 hectares	4.4 hectares

Question 2

The following graph shows the velocity of two cars at different times.

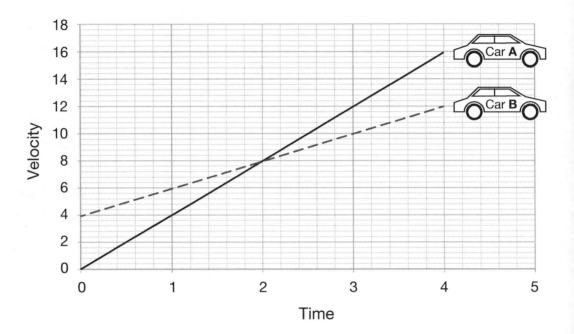

How much greater is the acceleration of Car A than the acceleration of Car B?

Acceleration (m/s2) = Change in velocity (m/s2) ÷ Change in time (s)

A	B	C	D
2 m/s2	4 m/s2	6 m/s2	8 m/s2

Question 3

What is 33.6 x 24.5?

A	B	C	D
842.3	823.5	823.2	842.4

Question 4

The Siberian tiger population in Country A is 60% of the Siberian tiger population in Country B. The population of Siberian tigers in Country C is 50% of that in Country A.

If the Siberian tiger population in Country C is 420, what is the Siberian tiger population in Country B?

A	B	C	D
1,400	1,200	1,000	1,600

Question 5

The graph shows respondents' responses when asked what their most frequent form of technological communication was.

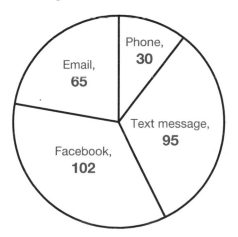

Responses when asked what their most frequent technological communication tool was

Among the respondents, 75% of all respondents said that it was easier to get in touch with someone through technological communications based on *convenience*. How many people said that it was easier to use technological communications based on convenience?

A	B	C	D
212	119	227	219

Question 6

In a survey, people had to choose either A, B, C or D.

The percentages for A, C and D are shown below.

A	B	C	D
25%		30%	15%

320 people chose A. How many people chose option B?

A	B	C	D
215	384	429	502

Question 7

Below is a table representing the number of deliveries in March 2014.

Delivery Area	Truck A	Truck B	Truck C	Truck D	Truck E
Cardiff	315	255	354	269	466
Manchester	759	436	157	357	143
Brighton	135	764	125	456	421
Dover	355	874	477	258	465
Portsmouth	551	668	567	776	904

It is expected that there will be a 35% increase in demand for deliveries in March the following year, and a new truck will need to join the company.

If the new truck covers all of the new deliveries, how many deliveries in total will the new truck have to deliver next March? Rounded up to the nearest whole number.

A	B	C	D
3,250	3,350	3,790	3,957

Question 8

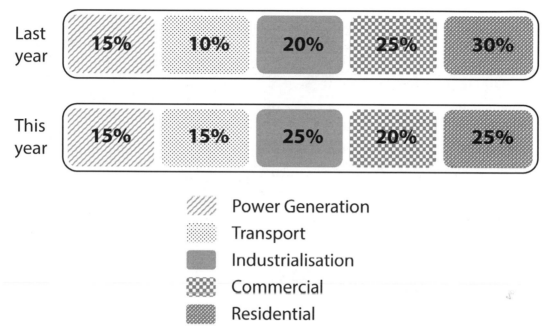

Carbon Emissions

Last year	15% · 10% · 20% · 25% · 30%
This year	15% · 15% · 25% · 20% · 25%

Power Generation
Transport
Industrialisation
Commercial
Residential

If transport emitted 6 million tons this year, and industrial emissions are the same as last year, what were the commercial emissions last year?

A	B	C	D	E
11.5 million ton	10 million tons	3 million tons	12.5 million tons	8.5 million tons

Question 9

Below is a table representing the income of industries (in billions of pounds) over a five year period.

	Year 1	Year 2	Year 3	Year 4	Year 5
Financing	65	82	93	100	112
Telecommunications	18	21	27	34	38
Engineering	37	58	60	64	68
Agriculture	26	26	30	30	55
Media	59	60	72	78	75
Manufacturing	33	38	41	30	27
Transportation	48	48	49	56	60

Which industry had the largest increase in amount of income between Year 2 and Year 3?

A	B	C	D	E
Financing	Transportation	Media	Agriculture	Engineering

Question 10

Below is a table of the total staff at Company A (Staff Distribution).

	HR	Sales	Finance	Media	Distribution	TOTAL(%)
Year 1	21%	8%	19%	32%	20%	100
Year 2	28%	11%	17%	28%	16%	100
Year 3	16%	21%	19%	26%	18%	100
Year 4	14%	29%	21%	14%	22%	100
Year 5	4%	9%	25%	38%	24%	100
Year 6	20%	27%	25%	12%	16%	100

In Year 4, there were 406 people employed in Finance. How many people in total were employed in Year 4 in the department of Sales? To the nearest whole person.

Answer

Question 11

In May, Jamie worked a total of 106 hours, in June he worked 118 hours – by what percentage did Jamie's working hours increase in June? Rounded to the nearest whole number.

A	B	C	D
11% decrease	12% increase	12% decrease	11% increase

Question 12

What is 17 multiplied by 4 divided by 4?

A	B	C	D
17	21	13	11

Question 13

Which of the following fractions is equivalent to 8/12?

A	B	C	D
48/72	4/5	16/32	80/100

Question 14

Work out the angles for A, B and C.

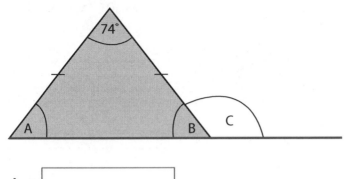

A = [   ]

B = [   ]

C = [   ]

Question 15

Multiply 6 by 7 and then divide by 3.

Answer [   ]

Question 16

Divide 120 by 4 and then multiply it by 5.

Answer [   ]

Question 17

What is 9/11 of 88?

Answer [   ]

Question 18

An English class of 28 have just sat a mock exam. The exam has 2 sections – Literature and Language. It takes approximately 6 minutes to mark the Literature section and 7 minutes to mark the Language section. Another 2 minutes is given to check each exam. How long in hours and minutes does it take to mark the English mock exam?

A	B	C	D
6 hours and 45 minutes	5 hours and 25 minutes	7 hours	9 hours and 10 minutes

Question 19

A function is represented by the following machine.

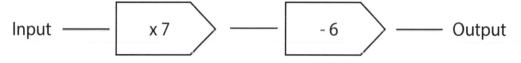

A number is put into the machine. The output of the machine is 309. What was the number first inputted into the machine?

Answer

Question 20

A function is represented by the following machine.

9 is put into the machine. The output of the machine is 126. What is the missing function in the second part of the machine sequence?

Answer

ROYAL NAVY RECRUIT TEST NUMERICAL REASONING – TEST SECTION 2 ANSWERS

Q1. C = 44 hectares

EXPLANATION = Work out the area of the whole shape: 1200 x 500 = 600,000

Work out the area of the missing rectangle (to make a complete rectangle): 800 x 200 = 160,000

So, 600,000 – 160,000 = 440,000m².

440,000m² in hectares = 440,000 ÷ 10,000 = 44 hectares.

Q2. A = 2 m/s2

EXPLANATION = (y final – y initial) ÷ (x final – x initial).

Car A = (16-0) ÷ (4-0) = 16 ÷ 4 = 4.

Car B = (12-4) ÷ (4-0) = 8 ÷ 4 = 2.

So, the difference between car A and car B is 2 m/s2.

Q3. C = 823.2

EXPLANATION = 33.6 x 24.5. The best thing to do is take out the decimal points, do the sum, and then add in the decimal point at the end. So, 336 x 245 = 82320. Now add the decimal point back in, you need to move the decimal point two spaces to the left (because there were 2 numbers after the decimal point in the original sum) = 82320 will become 823.2

Q4. A = 1,400

EXPLANATION = Siberian tiger population in Country C is 50% of that in Country A.

If country C is 420, Country A = 420 x 100 ÷ 50 = 840.

So, if Country A = 840 and is 60% of the population in Country B, Country B = 840 x 100 ÷ 60 = 1,400.

Q5. D = 219

EXPLANATION = first, you need to add up all of the respondents who took part in the survey: 65 + 30 + 95 + 102 = 292.

Next, you need to work out 75% of 292: 292 ÷ 100 x 75 = 219.

So, 219 respondents said they use certain technological communications for convenience.

Q6. B = 384

EXPLANATION = first you need to work out how many people took the survey in total: 320 (people who chose A) x 100 ÷ 25(%) = 1,280.

Next, you need to work out the missing percentage for B. 100(%) – 25(%) – 30(%) – 15(%) = 30(%).

So, B is going to be 30% of the total: 1280 ÷ 100 x 30 = 384.

Q7. D = 3957

EXPLANATION = add up all of the numbers in the table = 11,307.

To work out a 35% increase, 11,307 ÷ 100 x 135 = 15,264.45. To the nearest whole number = 15,264.

So, to work out how many deliveries the new truck will be making = 15,264 – 11,307 = 3957

Q8. D = 12.5 million tons

EXPLANATION = if transport emissions this year are 6 million tons – and equal 15% of the total – the overall total for this year would be 6,000,000 x 100 ÷ 15% = 40,000,000. So industrial emissions for this year would be = 40,000,000 ÷ 100 x 25 = 10,000,000. The industrial emissions are the same for last year, so to work out the overall total of last year = 10,000,000 x 100 ÷ 20 = 50,000,000. So the commercial emissions for last year = 50,000,000 ÷ 100 x 25 = 12,500,000 (12.5 million tons).

Q9. C = Media

EXPLANATION = you need to work out the difference for each industry from Year 2 to Year 3.

Financing = increase = 11

Telecommunications = increase = 6

Engineering = increase = 2

Agriculture = increase = 4

Media = increase = 12

Manufacturing = increase = 3

Transportation = increase = 1

So, the largest increase between Year 2 and Year 3 was the Media industry.

Q10. 560

EXPLANATION = in order to work out the number of people working in Sales in Year 4, you need to work out the total number of employees in that year.

So, 406 (number of people employed in Finance) x 100 ÷ 21 (percentage) = 1933.333. To the nearest whole person = 1933.

So, 1933 ÷ 100 x 29 (number of employees in Sales) = 560.57. To the nearest whole person = 560.

Q11. D = 11% increase

EXPLANATION = first we need to calculate the difference in hours between the new and original numbers. 118 - 106 hours = 12 hours. We can see that Jamie worked 12 hours more in June than he did in May – this is his increase.

To work out the increase as a percentage you need to divide the increase by the original number: 12 ÷ 106 = 0.1132

Finally, to get the percentage we multiply the answer by 100. This simply means moving the decimal place two spaces to the right: 0.1132 × 100 = 11.32. Jamie therefore worked an 11% increase.

Q12. A = 17

EXPLANATION = 17 x 4 = 68 ÷ 4 = 17.

Q13. A = 48/72

EXPLANATION = 48/72 is equivalent to 8/12 (both numbers can be divided by 6 to give you the original fraction).

Q14. A = 53°, B = 53°, C = 127°

EXPLANATION = a triangle contains 180°. So, 180 - 74° = 106°. Both A and B are going to be the same size (you will notice two small lines placed on both sides of the triangle, illustrating that they're the same size and length). So, 106 ÷ 2 = 53°. To work out angle C, a straight line has 180°. You've just worked out angle B is 53°, so 180° − 53° = 127°.

Q15. 14

EXPLANATION = 6 x 7 = 42 ÷ 3 = 14.

Q16. 150

EXPLANATION = 120 ÷ 4 = 30 x 5 = 150.

Q17. 72

EXPLANATION = 88 ÷ 11 = 8 x 9 = 72.

Q18. C = 7 hours

EXPLANATION = total time spent marking one exam = 6 minutes (Literature) + 7 minutes (Language) + 2 minutes (checking) = 15 minutes. So, 28 exams will take = 15 (minutes) x 28 (exams) = 420 minutes. Converted into hours and minutes = 7 hours.

Q19. 45

EXPLANATION = 309 + 6 ÷ 7 = 45. Remember, to work out the original number, you must work backwards. In order for you to work backwards, you must do the opposite to what the machine is telling you to do.

Q20. Multiply by 6 or (x6), or add 105 (+105)

EXPLANATION = 9 + 12 = 21. 126 ÷ 21 = 6. Therefore if you put (x6) into the equation (because you divided 126 by 6, you would put the opposite into the equation). 9 + 12 x 6 = 126. (Add 105 also works in the equation).

You have now completed the Royal Navy Recruiting Test.

The Royal Air Force Airman/Airwoman Selection Test
(RAF)

WHAT IS THE ROYAL AIR FORCE AIRMAN/AIRWOMAN SELECTION TEST?

The RAF Airman/Airwoman Selection Test is used to determine whether applicants have the skills and abilities required to work within the service. The test is ultimately designed to assess which careers in the RAF are most suitable to you. There are many different career opportunities available, and each one requires a different level of skill and intellect. The higher you score in your assessment, the more opportunities you will have at your disposal.

WHO NEEDS TO TAKE THE RAF SELECTION TEST?

If you are applying to join the Royal Air Force for any position or level, you will be required to complete the RAF Selection Test.

WHY DO I NEED TO BE ASSESSED?

The main purpose of the Selection Test is to establish which careers in the RAF are most suited to you. These tests are specifically designed to assess the key skills and abilities which are mandatory if you wish to join the RAF.

Psychometric tests are a useful way to decipher a person's level of intellectual, critical and technical ability. These tests evaluate a candidate's performance to determine whether or not a person is capable of handling the demands of a RAF career.

WHAT DOES THE RAF SELECTION TEST CONSIST OF?

The RAF Selection Test covers the following areas:

- *A Verbal Reasoning Test (20 questions to be completed in 15 minutes);*
- *A Numeracy Test (27 questions to be completed in 15 minutes);*
- *A Work Rate Test (20 questions to be completed in 4 minutes);*
- *A Spatial Reasoning Test (10 questions to be completed in 4 minutes);*

- *A Mechanical Comprehension Test (20 questions to be completed in 10 minutes);*
- *An Electrical Test (21 questions to be completed in 11 minutes);*
- *A Memory Test (20 questions to be completed in 10 minutes).*

The tests are usually carried out at the Armed Forces Careers Office and will be taken under strict timed conditions. Details of the time restrictions and number of questions per exercise will be provided in your recruitment literature. Your recruitment literature is key! Make sure that you take the time to read through the whole booklet so you are fully aware of what is required for the assessment.

TIPS FOR PASSING THE RAF AIRMAN/AIRWOMAN SELECTION TEST

- Undergo as much practice as you can. The more practice you undertake, the more competent you will become, thus improving your overall scores and performance;

- Focus on practising the questions you struggle with first. Tackling the questions that you find most difficult will ensure that your weakest areas have been revised and conquered;

- *Verbal Ability* – it is important that you brush up on your verbal reasoning skills. Working in the RAF requires an ability to communicate effectively and demonstrate precision, accuracy and intelligence;

- *Numerical Reasoning* – this will assess your ability to deal with numbers and sequences. Make sure that you have a *strong* understanding of basic mathematics. These should include: multiplication, division, ratios, fractions, percentages, areas, number sequences etc;

- *Spatial Reasoning* – you will be required to undergo a test that focuses on your ability to work with abstract shapes and images. The key to this test is to practice as many spatial reasoning questions as possible. TOP TIP: If you are not confident with this type of test, I would suggest drawing the images on a piece of paper, rotating the piece of paper, and visually work out where the shapes would be positioned;

- *Mechanical and Electrical Reasoning* – working in the RAF will require strong levels of technical and mechanical understandings. Make sure that you practice these questions until you feel confident with the different types of questions that may appear in your assessment;

- *Memory tests* – these tests are designed to assess your ability to work swiftly through large amounts of information. The memory tests require you to concentrate on information or images and memorise it. The key to these types of questions is to undergo as much practice in regards to memory. TOP TIP: Memory games are a great way to improve your performance;

- *Work rate tests* – these types of tests assess your ability to work quickly and accurately whilst carrying out routine tasks. These questions often appear difficult, but the more practice you undergo, the easier they become;

- Practice your speed as well as your accuracy. Remember, the tests are timed, so you want to ensure that you have answered a sufficient amount of questions in the time frame provided;

- Eliminate the most obscure answers first. This will save you time. By eliminating the answers you know to be incorrect, will narrow down the choices of possible correct answers.

WHAT DO THE QUESTIONS LOOK LIKE?

Below are example questions of the RAF Selection Test questions that you will have to undertake. Read through the example questions carefully before undergoing the testing questions.

VERBAL REASONING

EXAMPLE 1

Read the following information carefully and answer the following question.

Car A is black in colour and has 4 months left on the current MOT. The tax is due in 8 months' time. The car has no service history and has completed 46,500 miles. The car has had 2 owners.

Car B is red in colour and has a full 12 months MOT. The tax is not due for another 8 months. The car has completed 14,459 miles and has only had 1 owner. There is a full service history with the car.

Car C has no tax. The MOT is due to run out in 3 months' time and the car has no service history. The speedometer reading is 121,000 miles and the car, which is black in colour, has had a total of 8 owners.

Car D is black in colour and has 7 months left on the current MOT. The tax is due in 8 months' time. The car has no service history and has completed 43,000 miles. The car has had 2 owners.

Car E has 5 months tax. The MOT runs out in 7 months' time. The car, which is red in colour, has a partial service history and has completed 87,000 miles. It has had a total of 3 owners.

Question

You want a car that is red in colour and has a full service history with less than 100,000 miles. Which car would you choose?

How to work it out

- Make sure you read the passage carefully. Pick out the key details from the question and determine which car is most suitable;

- You can automatically rule out Car A, C and D because they are not red in colour;

- You can rule out Car E because it only has a partial service history, therefore the correct answer is Car B.

Answer:

Car B

NUMERICAL REASONING

EXAMPLE 1

Add these fractions.

$$\frac{5}{7} + \frac{3}{5}$$

$$\frac{5}{7} \times \frac{3}{5} = \frac{25 + 21}{35} = \frac{46}{35} = 1\frac{11}{35}$$

Crossbow Method:

- The CROSS looks like a multiplication sign and it tells you which numbers to multiply together;

- One arm is saying 'multiply the 5 by the 5', and the other arm is saying 'multiply the 7 by the 3';

- The BOW says 'multiply the 2 numbers I am pointing at'. That is 7 times 5;

- The answer is 35 and it goes underneath the line in the answer.

EXAMPLE 2

Subtract these fractions.

$$\frac{4}{7} - \frac{2}{5}$$

$$\frac{4}{7} \times \frac{2}{5} = \frac{20 - 14}{35} = \frac{6}{35}$$

- To subtract fractions, the method is exactly the same. The only difference is, you minus the two numbers forming the top of the fraction, as opposed to adding them.

NUMERICAL REASONING

EXAMPLE 3

Multiply these fractions.

$$\frac{2}{3} \times \frac{4}{7}$$

$$\frac{2}{3} \times \frac{4}{7} = \frac{8}{21}$$

Arrow Method:

- Multiplying fractions is easy. Draw an arrow through the two top numbers of the fraction, draw a line through the two bottom numbers (as shown above) and then multiply – simple!

- Sometimes the fraction can be simplified, but in the above example, the answer is already in its simplest form.

EXAMPLE 4

Divide these fractions.

$$\frac{3}{7} \div \frac{1}{3}$$

$$\frac{3}{7} \times \frac{3}{1} = \frac{3}{7} \times \frac{3}{1} = \frac{9}{7} = 1\frac{2}{7}$$

- Most people think that dividing fractions is difficult. It's not! It's actually relatively simple if you have mastered multiplying fractions.

- Mathematicians realised that if you turned the second fraction upside down (as in the above example), and then change the 'divide' sum to a 'multiply', you will get the correct answer every time!

WORK RATE

EXAMPLE 1

Which of the answers below is an alternative code for **563**?

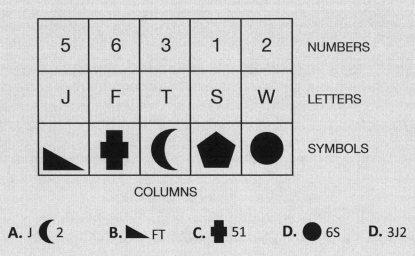

| 5 | 6 | 3 | 1 | 2 | NUMBERS |

COLUMNS

A. J ☾ 2   **B.** ◣ FT   **C.** ✚ 51   **D.** ● 6S   **D.** 3J2

How to work it out

- You will be given a code consisting of numbers, letters or symbols. Your task is to look at the 5 provided alternatives, and decide which one uses the SAME columns as the original code;

- As you can see in the above example, 563 uses the 1st column, the 2nd column and the 3rd column (in that order). So the code must use these columns in order in which they appear;

- You can see that answer B has the same code as 563. The triangle is taken from the 1st column, the 'F' is taken from the 2nd column and the 'T' is taken from the 3rd column.

Answer

B. ◣ FT

Things to remember:

- Make sure you pay careful attention to which columns are being used;

- I would suggest numbering the columns used (i.e. 1st, 2nd, 3rd), so when it comes to working out which answer is correct, you know which columns are being used.

SPATIAL REASONING

EXAMPLE 1

Take a look at the following 3 shapes. Note the letter on the side of each shape.

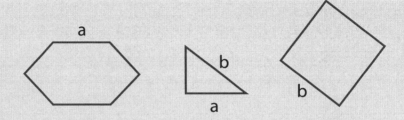

Join all of the 3 shapes together with the corresponding letters to make the following shape:

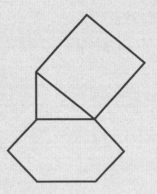

- Remember, for this type of question, you must use the letters to determine where each of the shapes will be positioned. The letters will refer to the side of a shape, which will then need to be connected to the side of another shape which also contains that letter.

Things to remember:

- The definition of spatial reasoning is as follows:

"The ability to interpret and make drawings from mental images and visualise movement or change in those images".

- Sketch out the individual shapes and then piece them together (like a jigsaw); this will allow you to visualise where each shape will be positioned;

- The more you practice these types of questions, the more competent you will become at working through them, and you will not have to rely on drawing the shapes out each time.

MECHANICAL COMPREHENSION

EXAMPLE 1

If the pulley is fixed, then the force required is equal to the weight. A simple way to work out how to calculate the force that is required, is to divide the weight by the number of sections of rope supporting it.

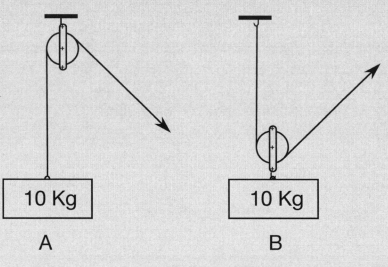

A   B

Diagram A = there is only one section of rope supporting the weight, therefore this can be worked out by = 10 ÷ 1 = 10.

Diagram B = there are two ropes supporting the weight, therefore this can be worked out by: 10 (weight) ÷ 2 (number of ropes supporting the weight) = 5.

MECHANICAL COMPREHENSION

EXAMPLE 2

When springs are arranged in a series, each spring can be the subject of the force applied. If the springs are arranged in a parallel line, the force is divided equally between them.

No Force Applied

Tension Applied

Compression Applied

No Force Applied

MECHANICAL COMPREHENSION

EXAMPLE 3

If the gears are connected by a chain or belt, then the gears will all move in the same direction.

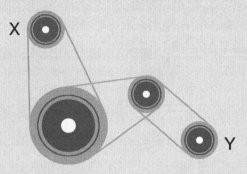

If the gears are touching, then adjacent gears move in the opposite direction. In the example below, X and Y will move in opposite directions.

ELECTRICAL COMPREHENSION

EXAMPLE 1

It is important that you are able to differentiate between series circuits, and parallel circuits. To distinguish between these two types of circuits, you should remember the following points:

- If there are no branches, then it is a **series** circuit;
- If there are branches, it is a **parallel** circuit.

Fairy lights

Series circuits can be described using the example of fairy lights. It is an electrical circuit in which the devices are connected end-to-end. It only has one path of flow.

Any break in the series of lights, results in no flow of electricity. In other words, if one light in the sequence breaks, the others will stop working.

Homes

Parallel circuits means more than one path of flow.

For example, in order to use multiple devices in your home, you use multiple paths of wiring that connects to an electrical circuit. This allows you to continue watching TV whilst turning off the lights.

ELECTRICAL COMPREHENSION

EXAMPLE 2

Electricity is a form of energy. You need to be fully aware of the dangers involved when using electrical components.

Below is a list of examples of ways in which you can be electrocuted if you are not careful when handling electricity:

- Pushing objects into plug sockets;
- Water touching an electrical compliance;
- Damaged wiring;
- Incorrect wiring;
- Overheated cables and plug sockets;
- Frayed cables.

Open Switch	Closed Switch	Capacitor	Lamp
Ammeter	Resistor	Voltmeter	Cell
Diode	Fuse	Battery	Variable Resistor
Light Emitting Diode	Thermistor	Light Dependent Resistor	Buzzer
Ohmmeter	Heater	Inductor	Transformer

ELECTRICAL COMPREHENSION

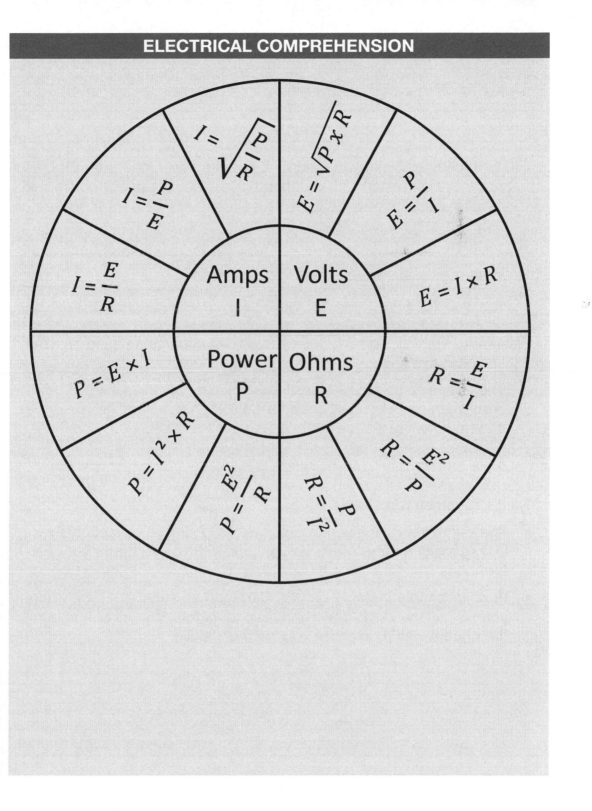

MEMORY TEST

EXAMPLE 1

W	E	Q	X	R	E

Study the sequence of letters for one minute only. Once the minute is up, cover the sequence with your hand or a sheet of paper, and answer the following question:

Question

How many letter E's were there in the sequence?

- The key to these types of questions is to memorise the whole sequence. The sequence will be removed after a set period of time, after which you will be required to answer questions based on what you have just seen;

- The answer to the above question is obvious, because the sequence is still there, so when you practice, be sure to cover up the sequence after a minute to ensure your performance is improved.

Things to remember:

- The key to improving your memory skills is simple – practice! Practice as many memory tests as you possibly can, to better your performance;

- Practice simple memory games! Card games such as *'Pairs'* where you face all the cards down and have to match up pairs of numbers, are a great way to improve your memory skills.

RAF SELECTION TEST – VERBAL REASONING

TEST SECTION 1

You have 30 minutes in which to complete the 21 questions. Please note that the time limit placed on this exercise will not be the same as the one set during the real RAF Selection Test.

FLAT A is located in a town. It is 12 miles from the nearest train station. It has 2 bedrooms and is located on the ground floor. The monthly rental is £450 and the council tax is £50 per month. The lease is for 6 months.

FLAT B is located in the city centre and is 2 miles from the nearest train station. It is located on the 3rd floor. The monthly rental is £600 and the council tax is £130 per month. The lease is for 6 months and it has 3 bedrooms.

FLAT C is located in the city centre and is 3 miles from the nearest train station. It is located on the 1st floor and has 1 bedroom. The monthly rental is £550 and the council tax is £100 per month. The lease is for 12 months.

FLAT D is located in a village. The monthly rental is £395 per month and the council tax is £100 per month. It is located on the ground floor and the lease is for 12 months. It is 18 miles from the nearest train station. The flat has 2 bedrooms.

FLAT E is located in a village and is 12 miles from the nearest train station. It has 3 bedrooms and is located on the 2nd floor. The monthly rental is £375 and the council tax is £62. The lease is for 12 months.

Question 1

You want a flat that is within 10 miles of the nearest train station and is located on the 1st floor or lower. The combined monthly rent/council tax bill must be no greater than £600.

A – Flat A

B – Flat B

C – Flat C

D – Flat D

E – None

Answer

Question 2

You want a flat that has at least 2 bedrooms and has a combined monthly rent/council tax bill which does not exceed £450.

A – Flat A

B – Flat B

C – Flat C

D – Flat D

E – Flat E

Answer

Question 3

You want a flat that has a combined monthly rent/council tax bill that is not in excess of £600, is within 20 miles of the nearest train station, and has a lease of 6 months.

A – Flat A

B – Flat B

C – Flats A or D

D – Flats A or E

E – Flats C or D

Answer

Barry and Bill work at their local supermarket in the town of Whiteman. Barry works every day except Wednesdays. The supermarket is run by Barry's brother Elliott, who is married to Sarah.

Sarah and Elliott have 2 children called Marcus and Michelle, who are both 7 years old. They live in a road adjacent to the supermarket.

Barry lives in a town called Redford which is 7 miles from Whiteman. Bill's girlfriend Maria, works in a factory in her hometown of Brownhaven. The town of Redford is 4 miles from Whiteman and 6 miles from the seaside town of Tenford.

Sarah and Elliott take their children on holiday to Tenford twice a year and Barry usually gives them a lift in his car. Barry's mum lives in Tenford and he tries to visit her once a week at 2pm, on a day he is not working.

Question 4

Which town does Elliot live in?

A – Redford

B – Whiteman

C – Brownhaven

D – Tenford

E – Cannot say

Answer

Question 5

On which day of the week does Barry visit his mother?

A – Monday

B – Tuesday

C – Wednesday

D – Friday

E – Whenever he can

Answer

Question 6

Bill and Maria live together in Brownhaven?

A – True

B – False

C – Impossible to say

Answer

Janet and Steve have been married for 27 years. They have a daughter called Jessica who is 25 years old. They all want to go on holiday together but cannot make up their minds where to go.

Janet's first choice would be somewhere hot and sunny abroad. Her second choice would be somewhere in their home country that involves a sporting activity. She does not like hill-climbing or walking holidays, but her third choice would be a skiing holiday.

Steve's first choice would be a walking holiday in the hills somewhere in their home country and his second choice would be a sunny holiday abroad. He does not enjoy skiing.

Jessica's first choice would be a skiing holiday and her second choice would be a sunny holiday abroad. Jessica's third choice would be a walking holiday in the hills of their home country.

Question 7

Which holiday are all the family most likely to go on together?

A – Skiing

B – Walking

C – Sunny holiday abroad

D – Sporting activity holiday

E – None

Answer

Question 8

If Steve and Jessica were to go on holiday together, where would they be most likely to go?

A – Sunny holiday abroad

B – Skiing

C – Sporting activity holiday

D – Walking

E – Other

Answer [   ]

Question 9

Which holiday are Janet and Steve most likely to go on together?

A – Sunny holiday abroad

B – Skiing

C – Sporting activity holiday

D – Walking

E – Other

Answer [   ]

You're twice as likely to die in a fire at home if you do not have a working smoke alarm. A smoke alarm is the most effective way of alerting you and your family to the dangers of a fire. This will give you precious time to escape and get out safely. They are relatively cheap, easy to get hold of and simple to fit. However, many people who have smoke alarms are in danger too. The alarm could be in the wrong place, there may not be enough of them, or the battery could be missing/not working.

Question 10

You are less likely to die in a fire at home if you have a working smoke alarm.

A – True

B – False

C – Impossible to say

Answer

Question 11

Many people who have smoke alarms are still in danger.

A – True

B – False

C – Impossible to say

Answer

Question 12

If the smoke alarm does not conform to the relevant British Standards, there is still the possibility that it will not work effectively in the event of a fire.

A – True

B – False

C – Impossible to say

Answer

Approximately two thirds of all domestic fires are cooking-related. That's a lot of fires. The kitchen is the single most dangerous place in the home.

Time and time again, it's the same problems that cause fires in the kitchens up and down the UK. If you know what these problems are, the chances of having a fire in the kitchen are greatly reduced.

Question 13

The kitchen is one of the safest places in the home.

A – True

B – False

C – Impossible to say

Answer

Question 14

Overheated chip pans are the biggest cause of fires in the kitchen.

A – True

B – False

C – Impossible to say

Answer

Question 15

It is the same problems that cause fires in kitchens up and down the UK.

A – True

B – False

C – Impossible to say

Answer

Electricity is everywhere in our homes, and plays an important part in our lives. It only takes one badly wired plug to prove just how powerful electricity is. The wires don't even need to touch for a spark to jump and a fire to start. You should never become complacent where electricity is concerned. Just because there's no flame, doesn't mean there's no fire risk. The major rule where fires are concerned is that you should not put people's lives at risk. Get everyone out of your home and call the Fire Service.

Question 16

Complacency is a must where fire is concerned.

A – True

B – False

C – Impossible to say

Answer

Question 17

Where fire is concerned, people's safety is a must. You should get everyone out and call the Fire Service.

A – True

B – False

C – Impossible to say

Answer

Question 18

You should never put water on an electrical fire.

A – True

B – False

C – Impossible to say

Answer

A row of terraced houses was partially destroyed by an explosion on the 17th of April 2014. Just before the explosion, a man was seen running back into his house. He had reported a gas leak to the gas board 7 days prior to the explosion. The following facts are also known about the incident:

- The smell of gas had also been reported by two further residents in the weeks leading up to the explosion.

- The police are investigating possible terrorist connections with one of the residents.

Question 19

A gas leak was reported to the gas board on the 10th of April 2014.

A – True

B – False

C – Impossible to say

Answer

Question 20

The explosion was caused by a gas leak.

A – True

B – False

C – Impossible to say

Answer

Question 21

The man seen running back into his house had already reported a gas leak to the gas board.

A – True

B – False

C – Impossible to say

Answer

RAF SELECTION TEST VERBAL REASONING – TEST SECTION 1 ANSWERS

Q1. E = none

EXPLANATION = you want a flat within 10 miles of the train station – this rules out answers A and D. You want a flat that is located on the 1st floor or lower – this rules out answer B. You want the rent and council tax to be no greater than £600 – this rules out answer C. Therefore, the correct answer is 'none'.

Q2. E = flat E

EXPLANATION = you want a flat that has at least 2 bedrooms – this rules out answer C. You want a flat with a combined cost for tax and rent to exceed no more than £450 – this rules out answers A, B and D. Therefore the correct answer is 'flat E'.

Q3. A = flat A

EXPLANATION = you want a flat with a combined cost for tax and rent to exceed no more than £600 – this rules out flats B and C. You want a flat that has a lease for 6 months – this rules out flats D and E. So, your remaining option is flat A.

Q4. B = Whiteman

EXPLANATION = Elliott lives in the town of Whiteman.

Q5. C = Wednesday

EXPLANATION = Barry tries to visit his mum on Wednesdays at 2pm. (It's the only day he has off from work).

Q6. C = impossible to say

EXPLANATION = you are not told whether Maria and Bill live together.

Q7. C = sunny holiday abroad

EXPLANATION = they are most likely to go on a sunny holiday abroad. They all mention a sunny holiday abroad as one of their choices.

Q8. A = sunny holiday abroad

EXPLANATION = Jessica and Steve are most likely to go on a sunny holiday abroad.

Q9. A = sunny holiday abroad

EXPLANATION = Steve and Janet are most likely to go on a sunny holiday abroad.

Q10. A = true

EXPLANATION = the passage clearly states that you are less likely to die if you have a working smoke alarm fitted in your home.

Q11. A = true

EXPLANATION = the passage clearly states that many people who do have a smoke alarm are still in danger too.

Q12. C = impossible to say

EXPLANATION = this statement is impossible to conclude from the passage. The passage does not mention anything in regards to British Standards, therefore you cannot make any assumptions based on the information provided.

Q13. B = false

EXPLANATION = this statement contradicts the passage. The passage highlights how the kitchen is one of the most dangerous places in the home.

Q14. C = impossible to say

EXPLANATION = the passage does not give any examples to the causes of these kitchen fires, therefore you cannot assume this to be an example.

Q15. A = true

EXPLANATION = the statement reinforces how the same problems are occurring up and down the UK, so therefore this statement is true.

Q16. B = false

EXPLANATION = this contradicts the passage as it states 'you should never become complacent where electricity is concerned'. Therefore this statement would be false.

Q17. A = true

EXPLANATION = this statement reinforces what the passage is saying, and therefore is true.

Q18. C = impossible to say

EXPLANATION = whilst it is common sense that you shouldn't use water to put out an electrical fire, it is not actually stated in the passage, therefore you cannot assume this to be true.

Q19. A = true

EXPLANATION = a gas leak was reported to the gas board on the 10th April 2014, so therefore this statement is true.

Q20. C = impossible to say

EXPLANATION = the passage does not confirm that the explosion was caused by the gas leak, therefore it is impossible to say.

Q21. A = true

EXPLANATION = this statement reinforces the passage's claim that 'a man was seen running back into his house. He had reported a gas leak to the gas board 7 days prior to the explosion'. Therefore this statement must be true.

Now move on to the Numerical Reasoning Test of the RAF Selection Test.

RAF SELECTION TEST – NUMERICAL REASONING

TEST SECTION 1

You have 12 minutes in which to complete the 20 questions. Please note that the time limit placed on this exercise will not be the same as the one set during the real RAF Selection Test.

Question 1

The two way table below compares pupils' results for GCSE English with GCSE Media grades.

English GCSE Grades	Media GCSE Grades								
	A*	A	B	C	D	E	F	U	Total
A*									
A		2	2	3					7
B		1	3	4				1	9
C			8	10	6	1			25
D				1		2			3
E								1	1
F									
U									
Total		3	13	18	6	3		2	45

The percentage of pupils who received a D grade in Media is approximately what? To the nearest whole number.

Answer [   ]

Question 2

Which of the following is not a fraction equivalent to 4/7?

A – 40/70

B – 24/42

C – 12/21

D – 8/14

E – 1/4

Answer

Question 3

What is 36/50 in its simplest form?

A – 1/5

B – 1/8

C – 12/20

D –18/25

E – 5/10

Answer

Question 4

What is 789.21 + 3415.25?

Answer

Question 5

What is 14% of 3658?

Answer _____

Question 6

A travel company sells 3080 UK holidays in 2014. It is expected that the number of sales will increase by 14% each year. Work out the number of UK holidays the company expects to sell in 2015. Round all numbers up to the nearest whole number.

Answer _____

Question 7

In England, if the petrol consumption per day dropped by 8% from 2014 to 2015, how much would the petrol consumption be in 2015?

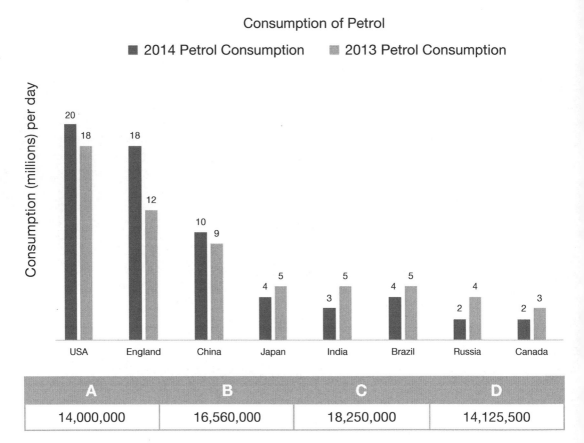

Consumption of Petrol

■ 2014 Petrol Consumption   ▨ 2013 Petrol Consumption

A	B	C	D
14,000,000	16,560,000	18,250,000	14,125,500

Question 8

Using the above chart, what is the percentage decrease for the USA between 2014 compared to that of the previous year?

A	B	C	D
15%	2%	1%	10%

Question 9

What is 40% of 360?

Answer

Question 10

What is 1/4 of 70?

Answer

Question 11

Which of the following is not an equivalent fraction to 1/3?

A – 2/6

B – 13/39

C – 3/6

D – 27/81

E – 9/27

Answer

Question 12

Sam falls asleep at 21:20, and wakes up at 6:15. How long did Sam sleep for?

A	B	C	D
8 hours and 55 minutes	9 hours	8 hours and 45 minutes	9 hours and 50 minutes

Question 13

Sandy buys a coat for £25.99, a new pair of shoes for £19.98 and a new handbag which costs £25.00. How much change will Sandy receive if she hands over £80.00?

Answer [   ]

Question 14

Michael needs to buy a new computer. He finds the computer online for £120. He goes into the store to buy it and finds out that there is a 15% discount if he orders today. How much would the computer cost, if Michael were to buy the computer today?

A	B	C	D
£98	£102	£18	£110

Question 15

Calculate how many acute angles are in the diagram below.

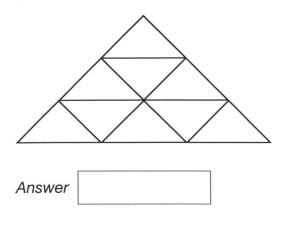

Answer [   ]

Question 16

Work out the following sum:

$$41 \times 8 = 1312 \div \, ?$$

A – 3

B – 4

C – 5

D – 6

Answer

Question 17

	Train 1	Train 2	Train 3	Train 4
Petersberg	6.45	7.04	-------	8.04
Hammersmith	7.00	-------	7.45	8.19
St Leonard's Station	7.12	7.20	8.00	-------
Mariweather	7.36	7.42	-------	8.30
Goldsberg	7.52	-------	8.19	8.48
Upperside	8.12	8.04	8.27	9.04
Franks Park	8.30	8.27	8.48	9.28

If I were leaving from Hammersmith, what train time is best to catch if I wish to arrive in Franks Park just before 9 o'clock?

A	B	C	D
7.04	8.04	7.45	7.00

Question 18

Using the table above, how many minutes slower does the 7.36 train from Mariweather take to get to Upperside than the 7.42 train from Mariweather?

Answer [   ]

Question 19

Using the table above, how long does it take in total if you were to catch the 7.04 train from Petersberg to Franks Park? Give your answer in hours and minutes.

Answer [   ]

Question 20

A school trip uses a mini bus to go to a museum. The price of the minibus is calculated per kilometre. Each kilometre is £1.86, and they need to travel 45 kilometres in total. If 9 people were to split the cost equally, how much will each person pay?

Answer [   ]

RAF SELECTION TEST NUMERICAL REASONING – TEST SECTION 1 ANSWERS

Q1. 13%

EXPLANATION = number of pupils who received a D grade in Media = 6.

Total number of pupils = 45.

So, 6 ÷ 45 x 100 = 13.333%. To the nearest whole number = 13%.

Q2. E = 1/4

EXPLANATION = ¼ is not equivalent to 4/7.

Q3. D = 18/25

EXPLANATION = 36/50 in its simplest form is 18/25 (both numbers can be divided by 2).

Q4. 4204.46

EXPLANATION = 789.21 + 3415.25 = 4204.46

Q5. 512.12

EXPLANATION = 14% of 3658 = 3658 ÷ 100 x 14 = 512.12

Q6. 3511

EXPLANATION = 3080 ÷ 100 x 114% (increase) = 3511.2. To the nearest whole number = 3511

Q7. B = 16,560,000

EXPLANATION = 18,000,000 ÷ 100 x 92(%) = 16,560,000

Q8. D = 10% decrease

EXPLANATION = the difference between 2014 and 2013 = 20,000,000 – 18,000,000 = 2,000,000. So 2,000,000 ÷ 20,000,000 x 100 = 10% decrease

Q9. 144

EXPLANATION = 360 ÷ 100 x 40 = 144

Q10. 17.5

EXPLANATION = 70 ÷ 4 = 17.5

Q11. C = 3/6

EXPLANATION = 3/6 is not an equivalent fraction to 1/3.

Q12. A = 8 hours and 55 minutes

EXPLANATION = if Sam fell asleep at 9.20pm and woke up at 06.15am, you need to work out how many hours and minutes he slept for.

9.20 to 05.20 = 8 hours, 5.20 to 06.00 = 40 minutes, 06.00 to 06.15 = 15 minutes

So 40 + 15 = 55, add the 8 hours = 8 hours and 55 minutes.

Q13. £9.03

EXPLANATION = 25.99 + 19.98 + 25.00 = 70.97.

To work out the change from £80.00 = 80.00 − 70.97 = £9.03

Q14. B = £102

EXPLANATION = 120 ÷ 100 x 15 = 18

120 − 18 = £102

Q15. 18

EXPLANATION = there are 9 small triangles, each of which have two acute angles (less than 90°) = therefore the total number of acute angles are 9 x 2 = 18.

Q16. B = 4

EXPLANATION = 41 x 8 = 328

1312 ÷ 4 = 328

Q17. C = 7.45

EXPLANATION = if you were leaving from Hammersmith, that means you need to focus on the second row of train times (don't count the train times from Petersberg). You want to arrive in Franks Park just before 9 o'clock, so you would need to catch the 7.45 train from Hammersmith.

Q18. 14 minutes slower

EXPLANATION = from Mariweather to Upperside on Train 1, it takes 36 minutes. From Mariweather to Upperside on Train 2, it takes 22 minutes. Therefore Train 1 is 14 minutes slower than Train 2.

Q19. 1 hour and 23 minutes

EXPLANATION = the journey time begins at 7.04 and arrives at its destination at 8.27. Therefore it takes 83 minutes in total to complete the journey. However, the question asks you to give your answer in hours and minutes, so the equivalent to 83 minutes is 1 hour and 23 minutes.

Q20. £9.30

EXPLANATION = in order to work out the cost per person, you should use the following method:

1.86 x 45 = £83.70

£83.70 ÷ 9 = £9.30

Now move on to the Work Rate Test of the RAF Selection Test.

RAF SELECTION TEST – WORK RATE

TEST SECTION 1

You have 8 minutes in which to complete the 20 questions. Please note that the time limit placed on this exercise will not be the same as the one set during the real RAF Selection Test.

Question 1

Which of the answers below, is an alternative to the code **G34**?

1	3	4
●	■	▄
G	R	T

A. ▄R1   **B.** 14R   **C.** ●R T   **D.** TR ●

Answer [   ]

Question 2

Which of the answers below, is an alternative to the code **CZF**?

Z	X	C
E	F	L
2	0	7

A. 72X   **B.** X02   **C.** LZE   **D.** F7L

Answer

Question 3

Which of the answers below, is an alternative to the code **NS4**?

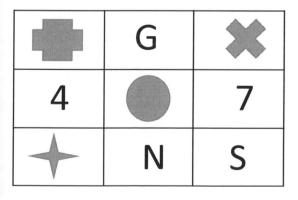

A. G7⬤   **B.** 4N7   **C.** ⬤✖7   **D.** G✖✚

Answer

Question 4

Which of the answers below, is an alternative to the code **1BM**?

★	★	☀	◆
3	1	A	K
M	P	0	B

A. ◆0A   **B.** PK★   **C.** P◆A   **D.** 30B

Answer [   ]

Question 5

Which of the answers below, is an alternative to the code **DP6**?

J	H	3	6
2	D	B	C
P	8	Q	9

A. 298   **B.** Q69   **C.** H2B   **D.** 829

Answer [   ]

Question 6

Which of the answers below, is an alternative to the code **BO3**?

H	⮕	5	⬅
6	B	⬇	O
Y	1	3	⬆

A. 1⬆⬇   **B.** 1⬅Y   **C.** 61O   **D.** ⮕51

Answer

Question 7

Which of the answers below, is an alternative to the code **JX8**?

X	◢	J	1
C	5	◣	8
◣	H	◖	◥

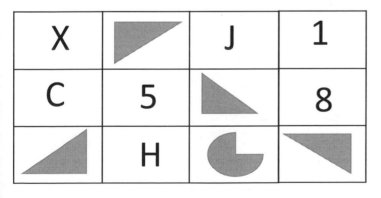

A. ◣C1   **B.** 8◖5   9 **C.** ◖HC   **D.** ◤◖◣

Answer

Question 8

Which of the answers below, is an alternative to the code **6SH**?

3	R	1	2	N	S
0	4	6	Y	Z	9
H	Q	V	C	M	7

A. 97Y   **B.** VZ3   **C.** 190   **D.** 3MC

Answer

Question 9

Which of the answers below, is an alternative to the code **QEA**?

↱	◖	▲	◄►
Q	9	5	A
1	B	E	4

A. 145   **B.** 1   **C.** ⌒B4   **D.** ◄►41

Answer

Question 10

Which of the answers below, is an alternative to the code **VFU**?

➡	♥	✹	8
F	5	U	V
🚫	9	✛	4
S	◣	Z	⬤

A. 5ZV   **B.** ⬤S9   **C.** ✛ 4S   **D.** 4S✹

Answer

Question 11

Which of the answers below, is an alternative to the code **KCH**?

A	B	C	D
Q	R	S	T
K	J	I	H

A. JHK   **B.** AIR   **C.** QSD   **D.** IHJ

Answer

Question 12

Which of the answers below, is an alternative to the code **GYL**?

Y	R	✖
U	●	B
✦	G	L

A. RUB   **B.** BLG   **C.** UR   **D.** RL✖

Answer [   ]

Question 13

Which of the answers below, is an alternative to the code **931**?

2	6	9
7	3	5
1	0	4

A. 361   **B.** 164   **C.** 407   **D.** 560

Answer [   ]

Question 14

Which of the answers below, is an alternative to the code **3MV**?

6	G	L
2	3	B
M	8	V

A. 82B   **B.** GB2   **C.** LG8   **D.** 28B

Answer [   ]

Question 15

Which of the answers below, is an alternative to the code **H4EC**?

5	H			P	L
			4		
E	R			K	C

A. KEP   **B.** R5K   **C.** 5L   **D.** PLCR

Answer [   ]

Question 16

Which of the answers below, is an alternative to the code **E7B**?

X	4	7	J
W	3	◺	F
E	P	◺	B

A. WX ◣   **B.** FBE   **C.** P3J   **D.** W ◣ F

Answer

Question 17

Which of the answers below, is an alternative to the code **DU1**?

⟳	E	Q	☀
⊘	7	W	A
1	D	⬌	U

A. 7A ⟳   **B.** 1 ⬌ W   **C.** AUW   **D.** ⬌ DU

Answer

Question 18

Which of the answers below, is an alternative to the code **HSP9**?

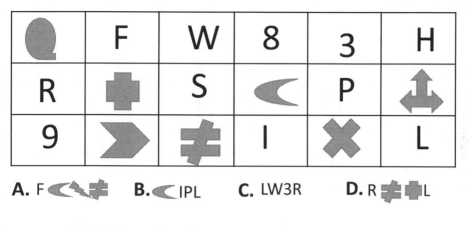

A. F◄◢✦ **B.** ◄IPL **C.** LW3R **D.** R✦✚L

Answer

Question 19

Which of the answers below, is an alternative to the code **P5X**?

⬆	H	5	X
T	✚	8	N
P	✖	0	⬆➡
4	★	F	1

A. TON **B.** ⬆8H **C.** 1F⬆ **D.** FTN

Answer

Question 20

Which of the answers below, is an alternative to the code **NUA**?

●	S	J	7
U	☀	N	A
1	T	◖	✛

A. ATS   **B.** J17   **C.** 71U   **D.** ☀UN

Answer [   ]

RAF SELECTION TEST WORK RATE – TEST SECTION 1 ANSWERS

Q1. C

Q2. A

Q3. D

Q4. B

Q5. D

Q6. A

Q7. A

Q8. C

Q9. B

Q10. D

Q11. C

Q12. A

Q13. C

Q14. A

Q15. C

Q16. D

Q17. A

Q18. C

Q19. A

Q20. B

Now move on to the Spatial Reasoning Test of the RAF Selection Test.

RAF SELECTION TEST – SPATIAL REASONING

TEST SECTION 1

You have 8 minutes in which to complete the 20 questions. Please note that the time limit placed on this exercise will not be the same as the one set during the real RAF Selection Test.

For the following 20 questions, the question is as follows: connect the shapes using the corresponding letters to complete the shape.

Question 1

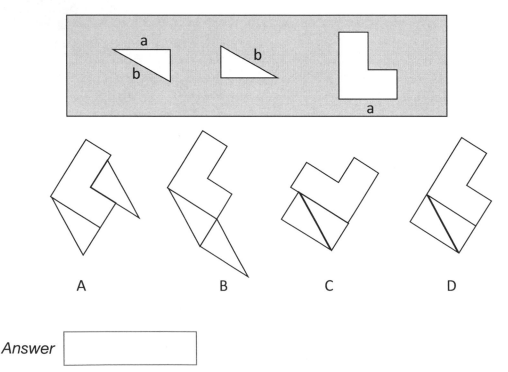

Answer

Question 2

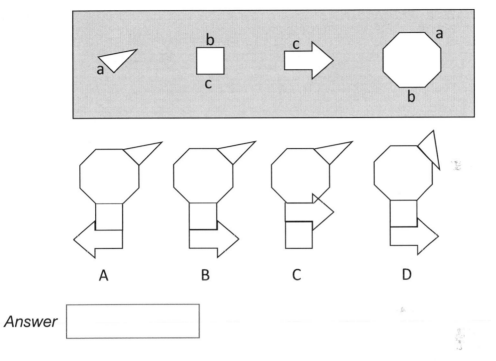

A   B   C   D

Answer

Question 3

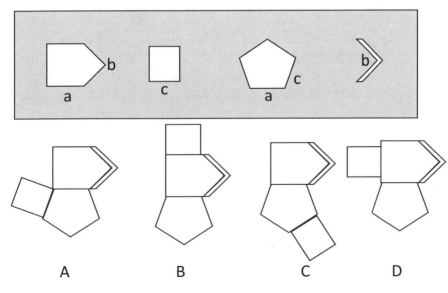

A   B   C   D

Answer

Question 4

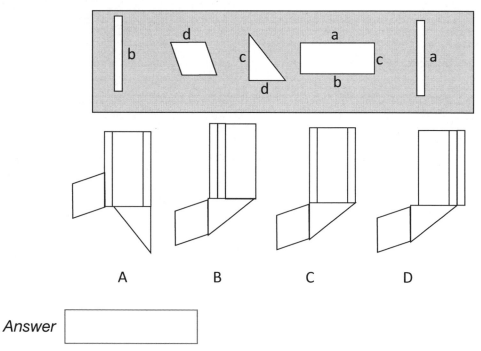

Answer

Question 5

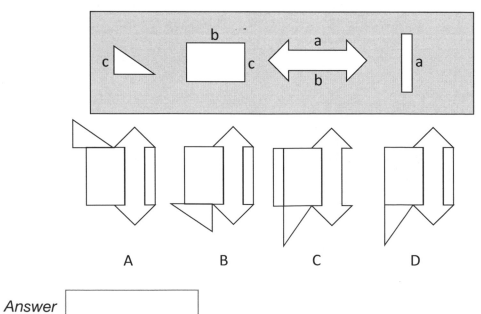

Answer

Question 6

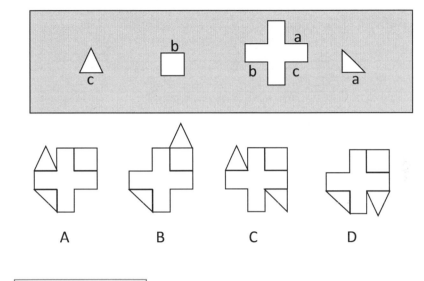

A   B   C   D

Answer

Question 7

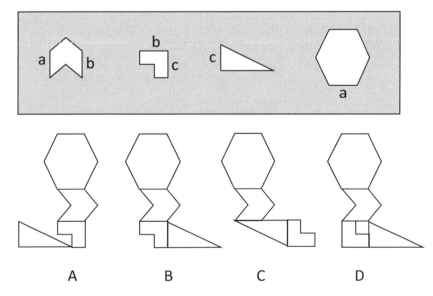

A   B   C   D

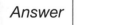

Answer

Question 8

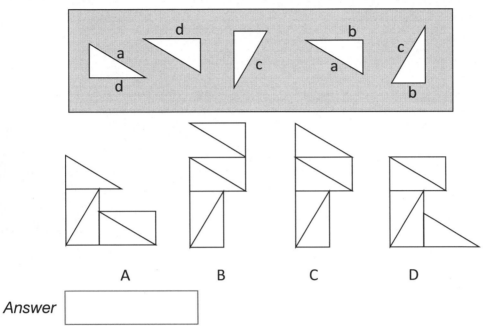

A   B   C   D

Answer

Question 9

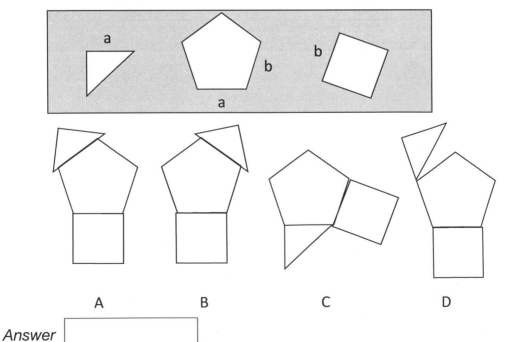

A   B   C   D

Answer

Question 10

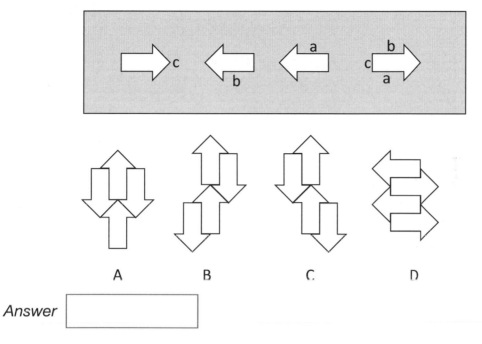

A   B   C   D

Answer

Question 11

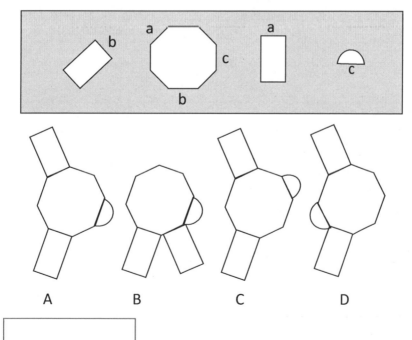

A   B   C   D

Answer

Question 12

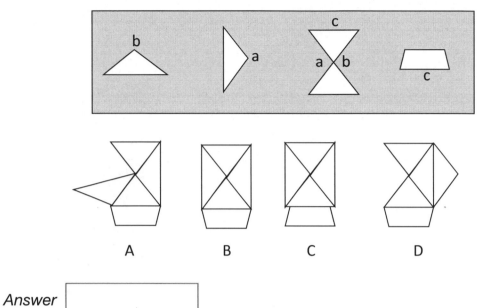

Answer

Question 13

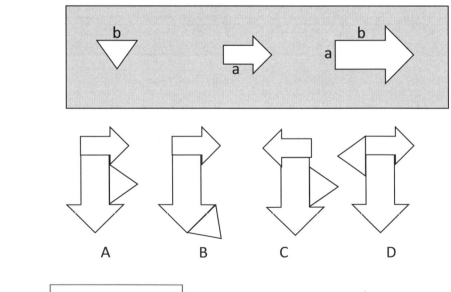

Answer

Question 14

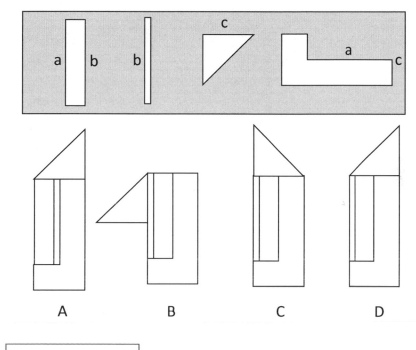

Answer _____

Question 15

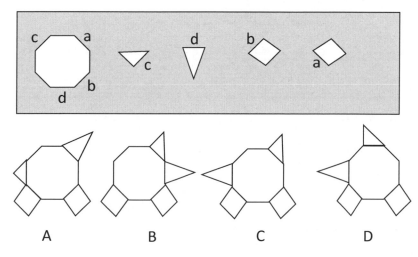

Answer _____

Question 16

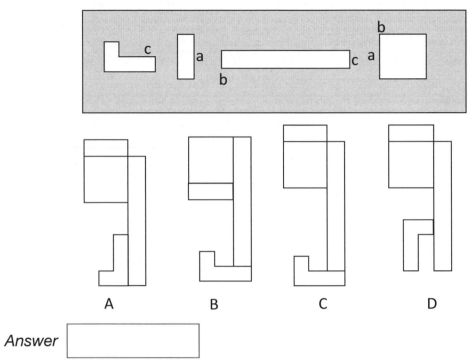

Answer [   ]

Question 17

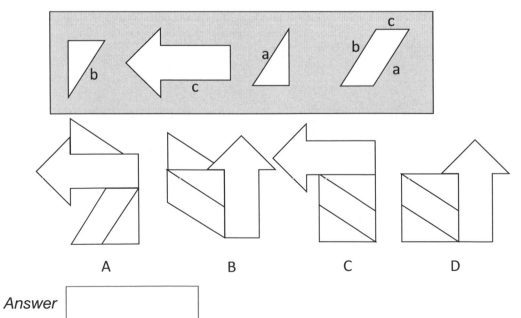

Answer [   ]

Question 18

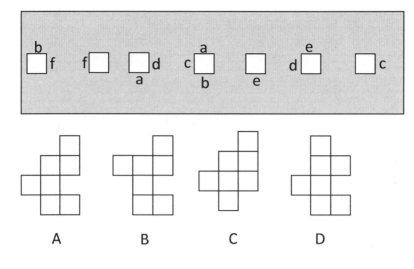

A B C D

Answer

Question 19

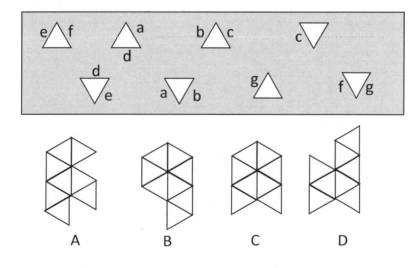

A B C D

Answer

Question 20

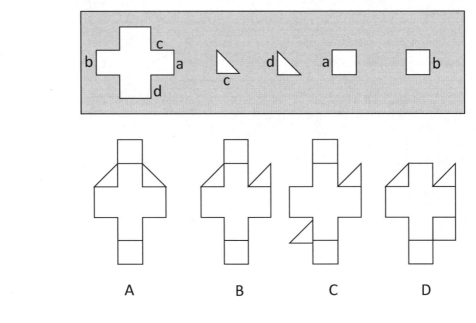

A   B   C   D

Answer

RAF SELECTION TEST SPATIAL REASONING – TEST SECTION 1 ANSWERS

Q1. D

Q2. B

Q3. A

Q4. C

Q5. D

Q6. A

Q7. B

Q8. C

Q9. C

Q10. A

Q11. A

Q12. B

Q13. A

Q14. D

Q15. C

Q16. C

Q17. D

Q18. A

Q19. C

Q20. B

Now move on to the Mechanical Comprehension Test of the RAF Selection Test.

RAF SELECTION TEST – MECHANICAL COMPREHENSION

TEST SECTION 1

You have 12 minutes in which to complete the 20 questions. Please note that the time limit placed on this exercise will not be the same as the one set during the real RAF Selection Test.

Question 1

Which load weighs less?

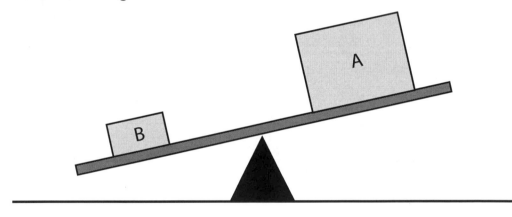

Answer

Question 2

At which point will the beam balance?

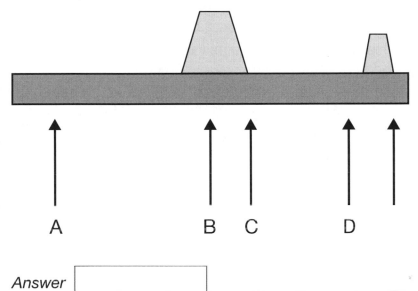

Answer [   ]

Question 3

Which post is carrying the greatest load?

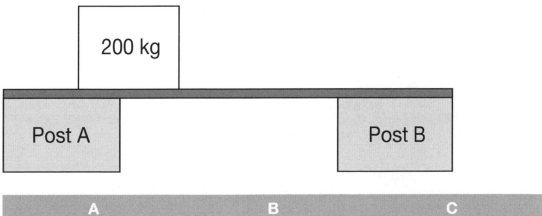

A	B	C
Post A	Post B	Both the same

Question 4

The following four containers are filled with clean water to the same level, which is 2 metres in height. If you measured the pressure at the bottom of each container once filled with water, which container would register the highest reading? If you think the reading would be the same for each container then your answer should be E.

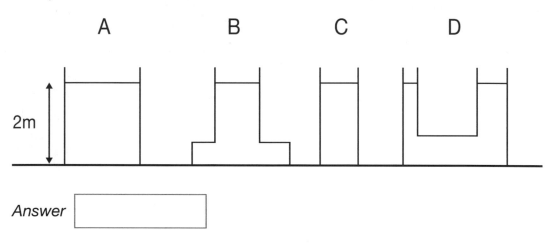

Answer

Question 5

If cog A turns anti-clockwise, which way will cog D turn?

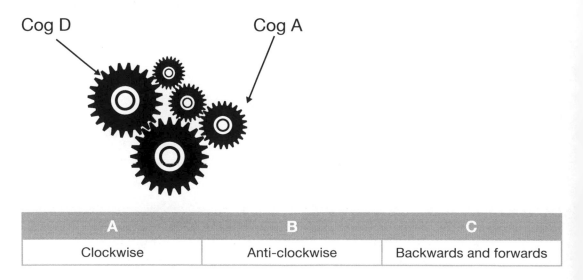

A	B	C
Clockwise	Anti-clockwise	Backwards and forwards

Question 6

Which weight requires the most force to lift it?

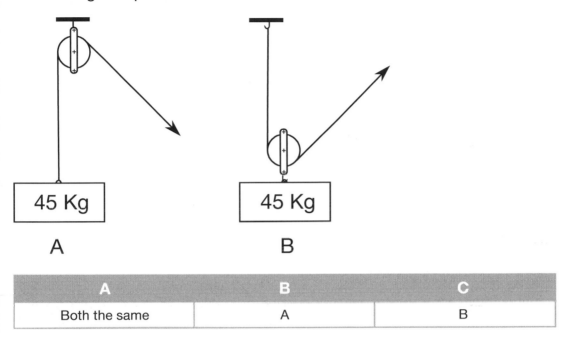

A	B	C
Both the same	A	B

Question 7

If wheel A is three times the diameter of wheel B and it rotates at 35rpm, what speed will wheel B rotate at?

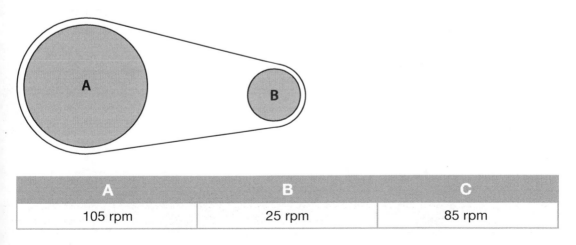

A	B	C
105 rpm	25 rpm	85 rpm

Question 8

On which pole is there the least pressure?

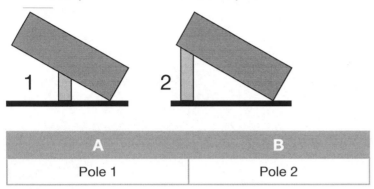

A	B
Pole 1	Pole 2

Question 9

If input effort is 750 ft.lb, what output effort will be produced by a machine with a mechanical advantage of 3?

Answer

Question 10

In the diagram, two wheels attached by a belt drive have the ratio of 3 : 1. The smaller wheel has a 10cm circumference. How fast would the smaller wheel turn if the larger wheel turned at a rate of 450 rpm.

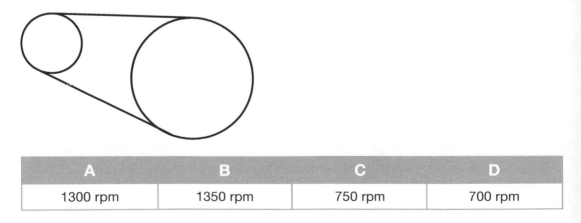

A	B	C	D
1300 rpm	1350 rpm	750 rpm	700 rpm

Question 11

How much force is required to lift the weights?

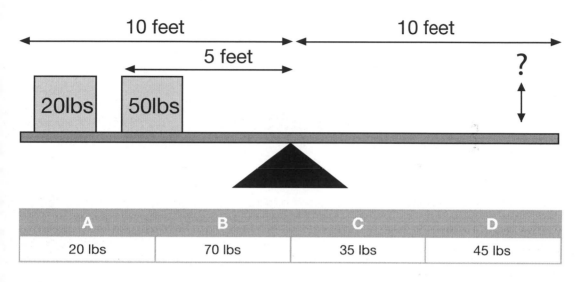

A	B	C	D
20 lbs	70 lbs	35 lbs	45 lbs

Question 12

Which post is carrying the greatest load?

Answer [   ]

Question 13

What would happen to a balloon full of air if you were to place it 15 feet below a water surface?

A – The volume of the balloon would increase

B – The volume of the balloon would stay the same

C – The balloon would explode

D – The volume of the balloon would decrease

Answer

Question 14

Which of the following statements will increase the mechanical advantage of this inclined plane?

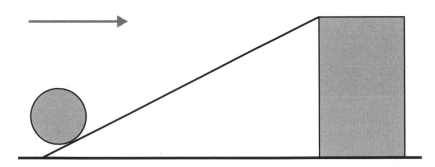

A – Shorten the length of the ramp

B – Make the ramp longer

C – Increase the slope of the ramp

D - Lessen the force acting at the arrow

Answer

Question 15

Which of the shelves can carry the heaviest load?

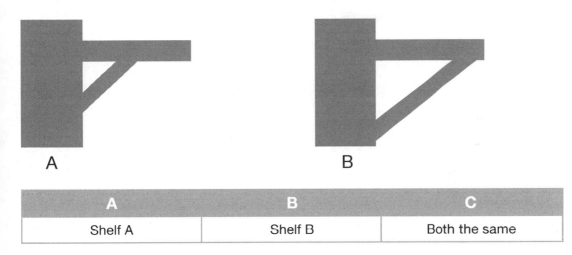

A   B

A	B	C
Shelf A	Shelf B	Both the same

Question 16

How much force is required to move the following weight?

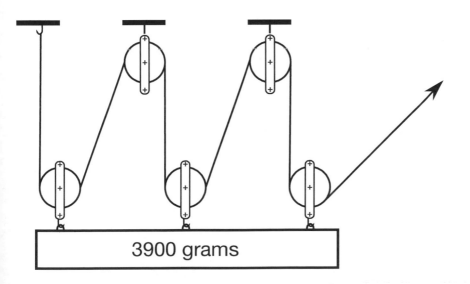

3900 grams

A	B	C	D
65 grams	1950 grams	650 grams	4000 grams

Question 17

How much weight is required to hold the load?

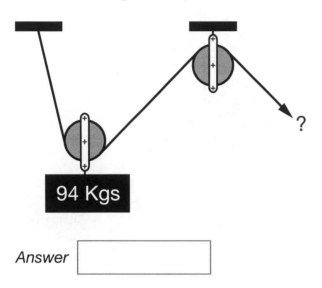

94 Kgs

Answer

Question 18

A valve is used to perform which of the following tasks?

A – Control the flow of a liquid.

B – Increase the temperature of a liquid.

C – Facilitate the evaporation of a liquid.

D – Decrease the density of a liquid.

Answer

Question 19

At what point would you need to place weight X in order for the scales to balance?

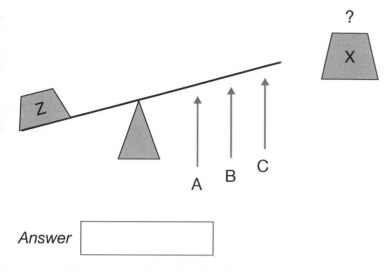

Answer [   ]

Question 20

Approximately how much force is required in order to lift the load?

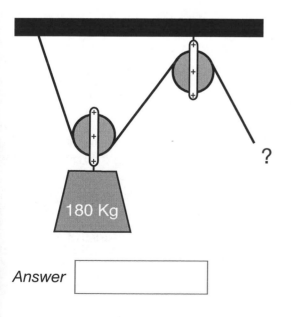

Answer [   ]

RAF SELECTION TEST MECHANICAL COMPREHENSION – TEST SECTION 1 ANSWERS

Q1. A

EXPLANATION = load A weighs less because the scales at point A are higher than they are for point B.

Q2. C

EXPLANATION = the beam will balance at point C. The bigger load needs to be balanced by the point of the beam. Only point C will balance the beam.

Q3. A = post A

EXPLANATION = post A is carrying the greatest load, because the load is positioned closer to post A as opposed to post B.

Q4. A

EXPLANATION = container A would register the highest reading.

Q5. A = clockwise

EXPLANATION = if cog A turns anti-clockwise, that means the cogs touching cog A will be rotated clockwise, and those touching them would go anti-clockwise and so forth. Therefore cog D will turn clockwise.

Q6. B = A

EXPLANATION = when answering questions where there is a single pulley system, if the pulley is fixed, as in A, then the force required to lift the weight is the same as the weight, i.e. 45kg. However, where the pulley system is not fixed and it moves with the weight (as is the case with pulley system B) then the weight required to lift it is half the weight. This means that the weight required to lift B is 22.5kg. The answer to the question is therefore B, as pulley system A requires the most weight to lift it.

Q7. A = 105 rpm

EXPLANATION = Wheel A is three times greater in diameter than wheel B, meaning that each revolution of A will lead to 3 times the revolution of B. Therefore, if wheel A rotates at 35 rpm, B will rotate at 35rpm × 3 = 105 rpm.

Q8. A = pole 1

EXPLANATION = pole 2 has the most pressure, because it is holding the whole weight of the object, whereas pole 1 is only holding half of the objects weight.

Q9. 2250 ft. lb.

EXPLANATION = 750 x 3 = 2250 ft. lb.

Q10. B = 1350 rpm

EXPLANATION = the large wheel rotates three times less than the smaller wheel. So, if the larger wheel is rotating at 450 rpm, this means that the smaller wheel must be rotating at a rate of three times faster. So, 450 x 3 = 1350 rpm.

Q11. D = 45 lbs

EXPLANATION =   f = (20 x 10) + (50 x 5) ÷ 10

f = (200) + (250) ÷ 10

f = 450 ÷ 10 = 45 lbs.

Q12. B

EXPLANATION = post B is carrying the heaviest load, because its surface area is larger.

Q13. D = the volume of the balloon would decrease

EXPLANATION = if you were to place a balloon full of air 15 feet under a water surface, the volume of the balloon would decrease. The pressure on the balloon from the water would press inwards, and this would cause the balloon to shrink in size, subsequently decreasing the volume of the balloon.

Q14. B = make the ramp longer

EXPLANATION = the mechanical advantage of an inclined plane can be worked out by dividing the effort of the distance by the resistant distance. In other words, the ratio of this formula must increase, which means making the distance longer i.e. lengthening the ramp.

Q15. B = shelf B

EXPLANATION = the shelf that can carry the most weight is shelf B. The bar holding the shelf up is positioned better in order to hold more weight. Shelf A has the diagonal bar positioned in the middle, and therefore placing a lot of weight on the shelf would cause it to collapse on the right side.

Q16. C = 650 grams

EXPLANATION = the weight of the object is 3900 grams. There are 6 sections (parts of the rope) supporting the weight. So, you need to divide 3900 by 6 to generate your answer. 3900 ÷ 6 = 650 grams.

Q17. 47 kilograms

EXPLANATION = 94 ÷ 2 (supporting ropes) = 47 kilograms.

Q18. A = Control the flow of a liquid

EXPLANATION = a valve is used to control the flow of a liquid.

Q19. A

EXPLANATION = in order for the scales to balance, the weight would need to be positioned at point A.

Q20. 90 kilograms

EXPLANATION = 180 ÷ 2 (supporting ropes) = 90 kilograms.

Now move on to the Electrical Comprehension Test of the RAF Selection Test.

RAF SELECTION TEST – ELECTRICAL COMPREHENSION

TEST SECTION 1

You have 12 minutes in which to complete the 20 questions. Please note that the time limit placed on this exercise will not be the same as the one set during the real RAF Selection Test.

Question 1

In the following circuit, if switch A and B closes, what will happen?

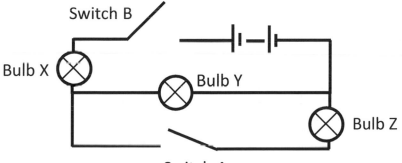

A	B	C	D
Bulbs X, Y, and Z will illuminate	Bulb X will illuminate only	Bulbs Y and Z will illuminate	No bulbs will illuminate

Question 2

In the following circuit, how many bulbs will illuminate if switches 1 and 5 close?

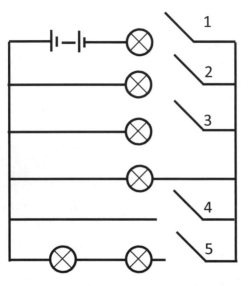

A	B	C	D	E
2	3	4	5	No bulbs will illuminate

Question 3

What is 'potential difference' also called?

A – Power

B – Voltage

C – Unit

D – Work done

E – Charge

Answer [   ]

Question 4

Which of the following is a definition of 'Ohm's Law'?

A – The relationship between current, voltage and resistance in an electrical circuit.

B – E = MC2.

C – An equation that converts energy into heat.

D – The total resistance in an electrical circuit.

Answer

Question 5

Which of the following statements is true in relation to parallel circuits?

A – The resistance is shared between each of the component connected in parallel of the circuit.

B – The voltage is shared between each of the component connected in parallel of the circuit.

C – The current is shared between each of the components connected in parallel of the circuit.

D – None of the above.

Answer

Question 6

What are the minimum and maximum acceptable values if a resistor has the resistance of 16 kΩ and can tolerate ±20%?

Minimum value =

Maximum value =

Question 7

Which of the following best describes what would happen if copper was moved across a magnetic field?

A – The wire would become magnetic

B – A voltage would be activated into the wire

C – The copper would melt

D – A current would be activated into the wire

Answer

Question 8

What is the total resistance of this network circuit?

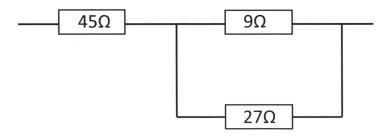

A – 36 Ω

B – 25.85 Ω

C – 51.75 Ω

D – 58.25 Ω

E – 60 Ω

Answer

Question 9

A battery with an electromotive force of 7 V produces a current of 11 A around a circuit for 6 minutes. How much energy is provided in the circuit within this given time?

A	B	C	D
32340 J	31440 J	310 J	4620 J

Question 10

Using the below Wheatstone bridge circuit, calculate the resistance of R3.

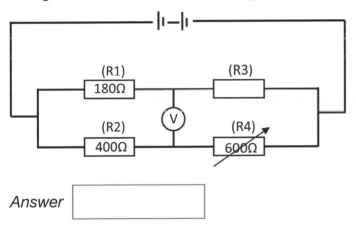

Answer

Question 11

A battery is measured to have the electromotive force of 6.2 V, and the internal resistance of 1.4 Ω. The battery is connected in a circuit to a resistor, which has the current flowing through it of 0.4 A. Work out the lost volts of the battery.

A – 0.56 V.

B – 1.6 V.

C – 0.16 V.

D – 5.6 V.

Answer

Question 12

Which of the following statements best describes the function of a capacitor?

A – Converts energy into sound.

B – Supplies the electrical charge.

C – Stores the electrical charge of the circuit.

D – A coil of wire which creates a magnetic field when current passes through.

E – Converts energy into light.

Answer

Question 13

In the following circuit, if bulb 1 is removed and the switch is closed, which bulbs will illuminate?

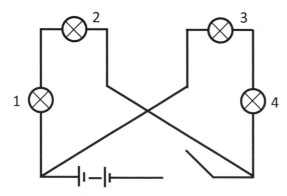

A – Bulb 4 will illuminate.

B – Bulbs 1, 2 and 4 will illuminate.

C – Bulbs 3 and 4 will illuminate.

D – Bulbs 1 and 4 will illuminate.

E – No bulbs will illuminate.

Answer

Question 14

An amplifier has an output of 2.15 V. If the gain is 320, calculate the input. Rounded to two decimal places.

A – 6.71 mV.

B – 6.27 mV.

C – 6.11 mV.

D – 6.72 mV.

Answer

Question 15

Identify the following electrical symbol.

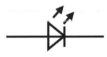

Answer

Question 16

Identify the following electrical symbol.

Answer

Question 17

Identify the following electrical symbol.

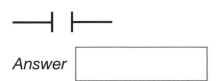

Answer

Question 18

Which two diagrams of the ammeters are NOT connected correctly? Circle two.

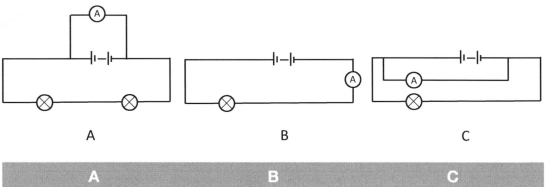

A	B	C
Diagram A	Diagram B	Diagram C

Question 19

35 kilovolts is the equivalent to which of the following?

A – 35 millivolts.

B – 3.4 volts.

C – 3000 volts.

D – 35,000 volts.

E – 350 millivolts.

Answer

Question 20

A current of 8.5 A passed through a circuit in 5 minutes. What is the quantity of electricity that is transferred?

A – 2970 C.

B – 2550 C.

C – 50 C.

D – 42.5 C.

Answer

RAF SELECTION TEST ELECTRICAL COMPREHENSION – TEST SECTION 1 ANSWERS

Q1. A = Bulbs X, Y and Z will illuminate

EXPLANATION = If switch A and B closes, that means the circuit is complete, and because the switches become 'on-switches', all of the bulbs will illuminate.

Q2. C = 4

EXPLANATION = if switches 1 and 5 were closed, 4 bulbs would illuminate. The bulb left of switch 1 would illuminate, the two bulbs left of switch 5 would illuminate, and the bulb on the fourth horizontal line would illuminate.

Q3. B = voltage

EXPLANATION = 'potential difference' is also another name for voltage. Potential difference is the difference of electrical power between two points.

Q4. A = the relationship between current, voltage and resistance in an electrical circuit.

EXPLANATION = Ohm's law refers to the mathematical formula involving the relationships found between the current, voltage and resistance within an electronic circuit.

Q5. C = the current is shared between each of the components connected in parallel of the circuit.

EXPLANATION = within a parallel circuit, the current is shared amongst each component that is connected in parallel.

Q6. Minimum = 12.8 kΩ, Maximum = 19.2 kΩ

EXPLANATION = 20% of 16 kΩ, or 16,000 Ω.

Step 1 = 16,000 ÷ 100 x 20 = 3,200.

Step 2 = Minimum = 16,000 – 3,200 = 12,800 Ω, or 12.8 kΩ

Step 3 = Maximum = 16,000 + 3,200 = 19,200 Ω or 19.2 kΩ

Q7. B = A voltage would be activated into the wire

EXPLANATION = a voltage can be induced into the wire if the copper conductor is moved across a magnetic field. Some of the electrons are free and therefore contain a force. The electrons are pushed downwards which leaves behind a positive charge. The electrons are negatively charged, so the charge in the wire has become separated which causes a voltage.

Q8. C = 51.75 Ω

EXPLANATION = in order to work out the total resistance of the circuit, you should use the following method:

Step 1 = $\dfrac{1}{9} + \dfrac{1}{27} = \dfrac{3+1}{27} = \dfrac{4}{27}$

Step 2 = So, 27 ÷ 4 = 6.75.

Step 3 = 6.75 + 45 = 51.75 Ω.

Q9. A = 32340 J

EXPLANATION = in order to work out how much energy is transferred, you should use the following equation:

Total charge transferred/charge = current x time.

So, 11 x 7 x 60 = 4620.

(volts x coulomb) = 7 x 4620 = 32340 J.

Q10. 300 Ω

EXPLANATION = in order to work out the resistance, you should use the following equation:

R1 ÷ R2 = R3 ÷ R4

Step 1 = R1 and R2 = 180 ÷ 360 = 0.5. So, R3 ÷ R4 needs to be equivalent to 0.5

Step 2 = R3 = (180 x 600) ÷ 360 = 300

Step 3 = you can double check to make sure that you have the correct answer by doing the following:

180 ÷ 360 = 0.5.

300 ÷ 600 = 0.5.

Q11. A = 0.56 V

EXPLANATION = in order to work out the number of lost volts, you should use the following method:

Step 1 = lost volts = 0.4 x 1.4 = 0.56 V.

Q12. C = stores the electrical charge of the circuit.

EXPLANATION = a capacitor is used to store the electrical charge of the circuit. It acts as a 'filter', blocking direct current (DC) signals, but permitting alternating current (AC) signals from running through the circuit.

Q13. C = Bulbs 3 and 4 will illuminate

EXPLANATION = only bulbs 3 and 4 will illuminate. If bulb 1 is removed, this will effect bulb 2 from illuminating because they run on the same path. Whereas, bulbs 3 and 4 are on a different path of wiring, therefore they are not affected, and are still able to illuminate.

Q14. D = 6.72 mV

EXPLANATION = in order to work out the input, you should use the following method:

Output ÷ gain = 2.15 ÷ 320 = 0.00671875

0.00671875 x 1000 = 6.71875. To two decimal places = 6.72 mV.

Q15. Light emitting diode (LED)

EXPLANATION = the symbol represents a light emitting diode.

Q16. Thermistor

EXPLANATION = the symbol represents a thermistor.

Q17. Capacitor

EXPLANATION = the symbol represents a capacitor.

Q18. A + C

EXPLANATION = diagrams A and C are NOT connected correctly. Diagram B is the only diagram that is connected correctly.

Q19. D = 35,000 volts

EXPLANATION = a kilo is equivalent to 1000 volts. Therefore 35 kilovolts is equivalent to 35,000 volts.

Q20. B = 2550 C

EXPLANATION = in order to work out the electricity transferred, you should use the following method:

8.5 x 5 x 60 = 2550 C.

Now move on to the Memory Test of the RAF Selection Test.

RAF SELECTION TEST – MEMORY TEST

TEST SECTION 1

> *Study the below sequence of letters for <u>one minute only</u>. Once that minute is up, cover the sequence with your hand or a sheet of paper and answer the following questions.*

B	I	O	P	B	C

Question 1

How many letters were there in between the letter I and the letter C?

Answer [   ]

Question 2

How many letter P's were there in the sequence?

Answer [   ]

Question 3

What letter was in between the letter O and the letter B?

Answer [   ]

Study the below sequence of letters for <u>one minute only</u>. Once that minute is up, cover the sequence with your hand or a sheet of paper and answer the following questions.

M	N	N	K	S	N

Question 4

What was the last letter in the sequence?

Answer

Question 5

How many letters were there in between the letter M and the letter S?

Answer

Question 6

What was the fourth letter in the sequence?

Answer

Study the below sequence of letters for <u>one minute only</u>. Once that minute is up, cover the sequence with your hand or a sheet of paper and answer the following questions.

X	a	C	C	p	A

Question 7

How many capital letters were there in the sequence?

Answer [   ]

Question 8

How many letters are between the letter X and the letter A?

Answer [   ]

Question 9

How many lower case letters (i.e. non-capital) were there in the sequence?

Answer [   ]

Study the below sequence of letters for <u>one minute only</u>. Once that minute is up, cover the sequence with your hand or a sheet of paper and answer the following questions.

e	E	e	V	E	o

Question 10

How many letter E's were in the sequence (capital or non-capital)?

Answer [   ]

Question 11

What letter comes fifth in the sequence?

Answer [   ]

Question 12

What letter comes last in the sequence?

Answer [   ]

Study the following grids for _10 seconds only_. Then turn the page and decide from the four options available which grid contains the collective group of coloured squares from the grids.

Question 13

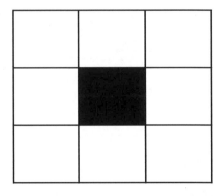

QUESTION 13 OPTIONS

A

B

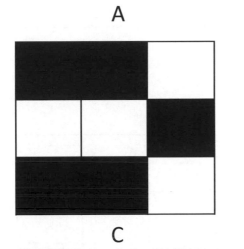

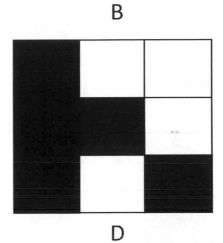

C

D

Answer

Study the following grids for _10 seconds only_. Then turn the page and decide from the four options available which grid contains the collective group of coloured squares from the grids.

Question 14

QUESTION 14 OPTIONS

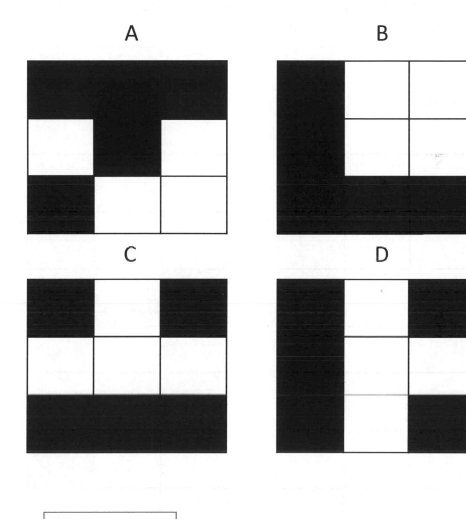

A   B

C   D

Answer

Study the following grids for <u>10 seconds only</u>. Then turn the page and decide from the four options available which grid contains the collective group of coloured squares from the grids.

Question 15

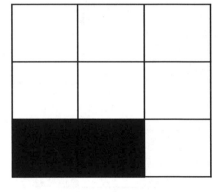

QUESTION 15 OPTIONS

A

B

C

D

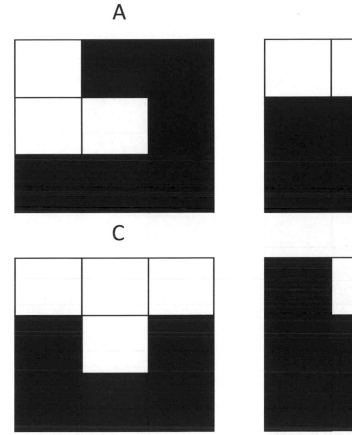
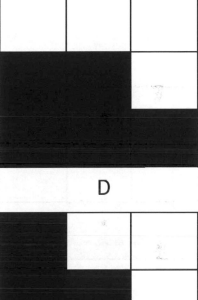

Answer

Study the following grids for _10 seconds only_. Then turn the page and decide from the four options available which grid contains the collective group of coloured squares from the grids.

Question 16

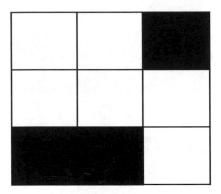
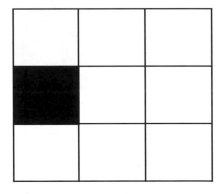

QUESTION 16 OPTIONS

A   B

C   D

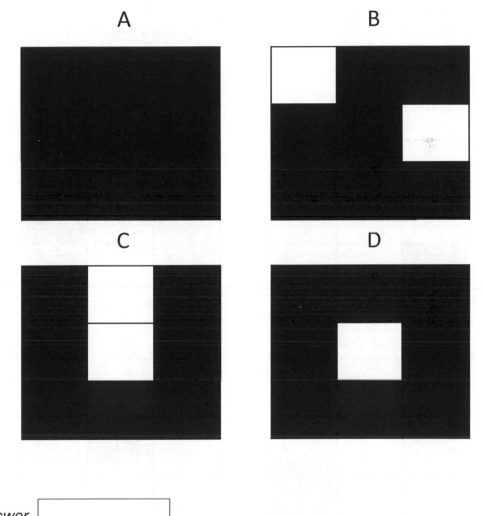

Answer

Study the following grids for <u>10 seconds only</u>. Then turn the page and decide from the four options available which grid contains the collective group of coloured squares from the grids.

Question 17

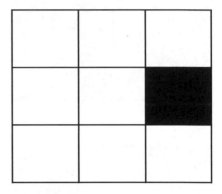

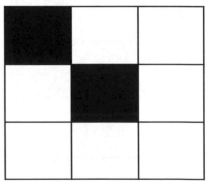

QUESTION 17 OPTIONS

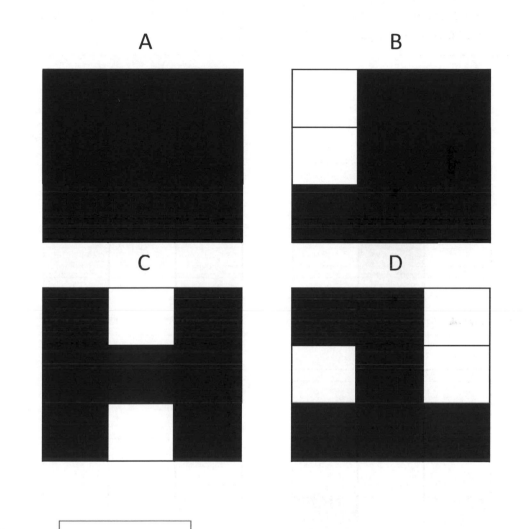

Answer

Study the following grids for _10 seconds only_. Then turn the page and decide from the four options available which grid contains the collective group of coloured squares from the grids.

Question 18

QUESTION 18 OPTIONS

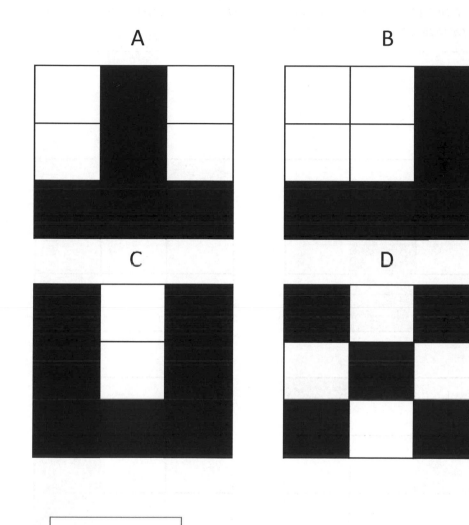

Answer

Study the following grids for <u>10 seconds only</u>. Then turn the page and decide from the four options available which grid contains the collective group of coloured squares from the grids.

Question 19

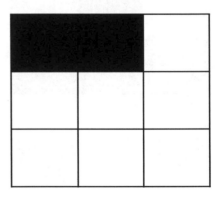

QUESTION 19 OPTIONS

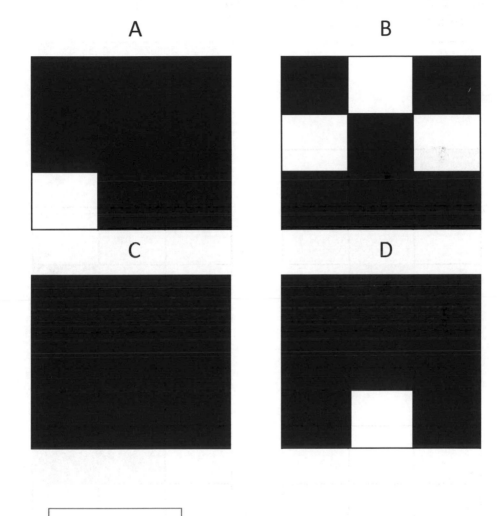

A

B

C

D

Answer

Study the following grids for <u>10 seconds only</u>. Then turn the page and decide from the four options available which grid contains the collective group of coloured squares from the grids.

Question 20

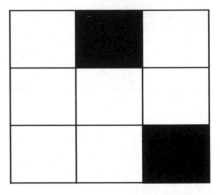

QUESTION 20 OPTIONS

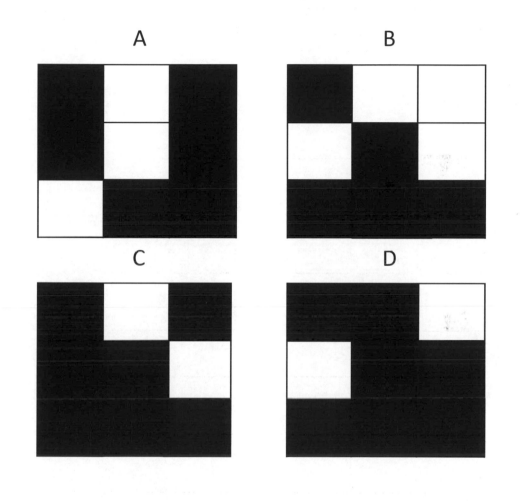

Answer

RAF SELECTION TEST MEMORY TEST – TEST SECTION 1 ANSWERS

Q1. 3

Q2. 1

Q3. P

Q4. N

Q5. 3

Q6. K

Q7. 4

Q8. 4

Q9. 2

Q10. 4

Q11. E

Q12. o

Q13. C

Q14. D

Q15. A

Q16. D

Q17. C

Q18. D

Q19. A

Q20. D

You have now reached the end of your RAF Selection Test.

A FEW
FINAL WORDS...

You have now reached the end of your Armed Forces testing guide, and no doubt will have a better understanding of the selection process for joining the Army, the Royal Navy or the Royal Air Force. We hope you have found this an invaluable insight into the psychometric tests that you will be expected to pass, if you are applying for a position within the Armed Forces.

As with any test, we believe that there are a few things to remember in order to help you perform at your best…

REMEMBER – THE THREE P'S!

1. **Preparation.** This may seem relatively obvious, but you will be surprised by how many people fail psychometric testing because they lacked preparation and knowledge regarding their assessment. You need to make sure that you have the best possible chance of succeeding. Be sure to do as much preparation as you can, to ensure that you are 100% prepared to complete the test successfully. Like anything, the more you practice, the more likely you are to succeed.

2. **Perseverance.** Everybody comes across times when there are setbacks or obstacles in the way of their goals. The important thing to remember when this happens, is to use those setbacks and obstacles as a way of progressing. It is what you do with your past experiences that will help to determine your future. If you fail at something, consider '*why*' you have failed. This will allow you to improve and enhance your performance for next time.

3. **Performance.** Performance is a great word! Your performance will determine whether or not you are likely to succeed. Attributes that are often associated with performance are **self-belief**, **motivation** and **commitment**. Self-belief allows you to recognise your own abilities and skills, and gives you the confidence to succeed. Believing that you can do well is half the battle! Being fully motivated and committed is difficult for some people, but nothing is gained without hard work and determination. If you want to succeed, you will need to put in that extra time and hard work.

Work hard, stay focused, and be what you want!

Good luck with your Armed Forces Tests. We would like to wish you the best of luck with all your future endeavours.

The How2become team

Get more books, manuals, online tests and training courses at:

www.How2Become.com